Tattered Banners

T0273487

Chevalier Guard.

Tattered Banners

An Autobiography

Colonel Paul Rodzianko C.M.G.

With a New Foreword by
Gary Saul Morson

PAUL DRY BOOKS
Philadelphia 2018

Author's notes:

My thanks are due to "Anita Leslie," my wife, for her invaluable help in writing this book.

To avoid confusion, the name "Petrograd" has been used throughout this book.

First Paul Dry Books Edition, 2018

Paul Dry Books, Inc.
Philadelphia, Pennsylvania
www.pauldrybooks.com

ISBN 978-1-58988-125-9

Printed in the United States of America

To the memory of men who knew how to fight

Contents

Foreword

COLONEL PAUL RODZIANKO'S VISION

Gary Saul Morson

MEMOIRS PLAY A large role in Russian literature. Radicals wrote the most famous ones. Alexander Herzen's *My Life and Thoughts* describes the experiences that led him to become a revolutionary and the key events of his career as a radical exile. There he ran a revolutionary press and exchanged ideas with what might be called Europe's "radical aristocracy": Garibaldi, Herwegh, Bakunin, and many others. The great Russian anarchist Peter Kropotkin gave us his *Memoirs of a Revolutionist*, which explains what led a natural scientist to become an anarchist. Quite popular in the last half-century of tsarist Russia were the recollections of terrorists: Vera Figner, Sergey Stepniak-Ktavchinsky, and Boris Savinkov. Reading them, we grasp how people who engage in assassination and commit indiscriminate murder thought of themselves.

Tattered Banners is another sort of memoir altogether. Its author, Paul Rodzianko, could not be further from the radicals. Here we catch a glimpse of the mindset and life patterns of Russia's highest aristocracy, the people on whom the crown, and later the liberal opposition composing the first Russian parliament (the Duma), depended. With his eye for detail, his taste for anecdote, and his sheer delight in the process of living, Rodzianko has created a delightful, if often sad, work.

He could not have been better connected. He romped in the Winter Palace, knew the royal family personally, and his own family took untold wealth for granted. His mother was a Stroganoff who inherited some of the family's fabulous jewels, second only to those of the Imperial family. He recalls that "the Empress Marie once laughingly asked mother, 'Do not wear emeralds the same night that I do. Yours make mine look pale.'" Grand Dukes and Duchesses attended his wedding, and one of them promised to be godfather to his first son. His uncle, Michael Rodzianko, became president of the Duma. Paul Rodzianko also knew the cultural, as well as the social and political, elite. During wartime, strolling down a hotel corridor in Warsaw, he meets his old pal, Russia's legendary opera singer Fyodor Chaliapin, "who was giving concerts in the packed city. That night he came to my room and sang for hours."

And what was the life of such aristocrats like? Unlike the aristocrats of England and France, Russian elites grew up speaking another language (or languages) fluently. Readers of Tolstoy's *War and Peace* will recall that at the beginning of the nineteenth century the elite spoke French better than Russian, which was typically used only to converse with the lower classes. In Rodzianko's time, the fashionable language was English, which is why novelist Vladimir Nabokov was bilingual. Rodzianko explains: "We spoke English before Russian and our infant memories were fed with tales of that far wonderful country . . . The Russian aristocracy was the most cosmopolitan in the world. We thought in Russian, spoke French and English between ourselves, and used German for technical discussions."

Also unlike their English and German counterparts, Russian aristocrats took special pride in living for the day. Rodzianko's father did whatever he wanted to do, "right away without any worry," while the family did not even know what their income was. "All that [accounting] was done by 'efficient German agents.'" Then there is the amazing story of his gluttonous Uncle Kotchubey, whom you could always find at the most expensive restaurants abroad. "Kotchubey had been very rich, but he literally ate away his fortune."

In exile after the Revolution—the only way he could have survived—Rodzianko recalls: "Writing this in the civilized serenity of modern England, I can hardly believe that from my bedroom window one could sometimes see bears going down to the lakeside to drink. Their pugmarks and those of wolves could be found in the morning." The English chased foxes, the Russians wolves! Animals, in fact, play a large role in this memoir, as they do not in more urban writers' works. Growing up, Rodzianko had tamed bears as pets. "Mishka, my own special pet, traveled with me in trains and slept in my study. Mishka . . . had a liking for beer, which he drank solemnly out of the bottle, sitting on his hind legs." One story testifies to Mishka's intelligence. "Mishka had watched her [the cook] in the yard throwing corn to chickens and then catching one to kill . . . Now, copying her, he sat down and rubbed gravel between his paws, giving the effect of corn. The idiotic chickens ran up and started to peck. Immediately he caught one and made off."

With his love of animals, Rodzianko took lessons, in Russia and abroad, on horsemanship. He eventually became a real expert, and, when in exile, could earn his living through his skill with horses. (He is also the author of *Modern Horsemanship*, originally published in 1937.) An important character in these memoirs is his favorite horse, Macgillycuddy, whom he procured in Ireland.

Rodzianko's attitudes reflect his upbringing. He reports that Russian officers, except when giving orders, would talk familiarly with their (mostly peasant) soldiers, asking with concern about their personal lives. He is well aware that any Englishmen would regard such condescending concern as an affront to his dignity, but in Russia inequality was taken for granted by all— or so Rodzianko imagines. He looks upon the peasants as lower beings whom he must care for. "Other countries seldom realize the happy, animal-like stupidity of the Russian peasant, who sleeps on his stove all winter like a bear." Indeed, for Rodzianko, the Russian aristocracy itself is childlike in comparison not only with their counterparts abroad but, more importantly, with the organized revolutionaries who would eventually take advantage of the aristocrats' genial weaknesses in order to seize power. For Rodzianko there is something loose, chaotic, spontaneous, and vast about Russia itself:

> It was not the debauchery of the upper classes that led to the downfall of the Russian empire, nor were the workers abused or the peasants bullied, nor was the Government retrograde . . . It was simply that Russia was too huge, too childish, too poorly organized to be able to go to war outside her borders. The very vastness that . . . defeated Napoleon proved her destruction. Enormous fronts, loosely hung together, sapped her best men and prepared the way for a revolution.

Of course, peasants were bullied and the government was retrograde, but Rodzianko has a point in mentioning poor organization and even childishness—if by childishness one means a lack of practical political acumen. The Duma was indeed given to rhetorical maximalism, a refusal to compromise, tolerance of terrorism, and a preference for high-sounding pronouncements over effective measures. Although Rodzianko does not say so, that was true of his uncle Michael as well.

For Rodzianko, the "new dictatorship" (the Soviet government) testifies to "how ridiculous and how weak is the mind of the masses. Then, as now, they think what their newspapers tell them to think . . . A few years of anti-war books and films have not changed the human mind, they have simply led to pacifists wanting to exterminate non-pacifists." The image of angry, armed pacifists is one of Rodzianko's most memorable, and is, of course, applicable far beyond Russia. When Rodzianko concludes, "Peace is now the excuse for war," we can anticipate the famous slogans in Orwell's *1984*: "War is peace. Freedom is slavery. Ignorance is strength."

Perhaps the most moving part of this memoir concerns Rodzianko's service as an officer with the British Army during the Russian Civil War. He was a staff officer who entered Ekaterinburg immediately after the Bolsheviks had evacuated it after murdering the tsar and his family. Rodzianko describes how he reconstructs what happened to them. Their rude male guards took pleasure in humiliating them. Not even the empress or grand duchesses could use the privy alone. When Rodzianko looks for where they are buried, he finds thousands of fresh graves with the locals explaining what had become an everyday experience: "Oh, just townsfolk shot by the Communists." He rescues their dog "Joy," the massacre's sole survivor.

For Rodzianko, the supreme virtue is courage and the willingness to fight. That is why the book is dedicated "to the memory of men who knew how to fight." Unfortunately, Nicholas II was not one of those. "My poor Emperor, if only he had been a little less kind . . . if only he had known to fight as well as he knew how to pray!" The educated classes were not much better: "though many had vision, none took up Russia's cudgel: impassive and mystic, they stood by, while the revolution swept their world away." Of course, other elites have been characterized by a similar suicidal tendency to place themselves above the fray.

In his conclusion, Rodzianko observes that "Europe is bored with Russian bestiality and cruelty, but half its tales remain unrecorded." Bolshevik cruelty was to increase more than Rodzianko could have imagined. In the twentieth century, Russia became an object lesson in what happens when intellectuals with a revolutionary ideology proclaiming they alone have the moral truth seize power. As a result, Russian memoirs detailing the country's experience are especially important. Rodzianko's is one of the more poignant. Above the English grave of the rescued imperial dog an epitaph sums up the aristocrat's experience: "Here lies Joy."

PART I

The Other World

CHAPTER 1

The Small Cloud

LONG BEFORE DAWN we were up, carefully trying on our black-and-gold tunics and our shining helmets topped with white horses' tails and the golden double eagle. Before the sky grew even faintly grey I and many other boys were struggling into our state uniforms, fastening the stiff red collars, pulling on polished boots and trying not to get our white trousers dirty. We thought only of ourselves and of our own small reflections, stiff and impressive in the half light; but what were the other visions, strange and wonderful, held by a thousand mirrors that May morning? For the proudest names of a proud country were gathered here. Swords and spurs were clattering and beautiful jewelled women, in flowing court dress, were already up and waiting when at last the sun rose, gilding the domes of the sacred city of Moscow. In the Kremlin, in the dark old rooms, one mirror's depths must still hold the imprint of a white face and lips that murmured "as Tzar and Judge of the Russian Empire, at the Judgement Day I may answer without shame." For Nicolas the Little Father of Russia on this day was to receive his crown.

I had been among those elected from the Corps des Pages of His Majesty to attend the ceremony. How many rehearsals took place within the old Kremlin walls, how many hours we stood to attention preparing for the great hour that had now arrived! Like a small walled city, the Fortress held two cathedrals, palaces, a

museum and buildings of all ages. A nervous little boy of thir-
teen, helmet pulled down over nose and careful to salute all Generals, I stood among the glittering throng that filled the Kremlin
as gold dust might fill an earthen box. The dark old Archangelski
Sobor, tomb of ancient Tzars, stood unsmiling by the Uspensky
Sobor, Cathedral of the Virgin's Falling to Sleep, where for many
centuries the Romanovs had been crowned. Here, only ninety
years before, Napoleon had dared stable his horses; horses in our
sanctuary that Russians thought beautiful as the skirts of God!
But now rows of captured French guns lined the inside of Kremlin's red stone walls!

A long procession of Marshals and Generals began to stream
down the Palace steps and along the raised platform which led to
the Uspensky Sobor. Troops presented arms and every one sang
the National Anthem as Nicolas II and his Empress appeared
and walked slowly towards the Cathedral, followed by the Grand
Dukes, foreign royalties and the Court. We pages stood hot and
rigid, watching them vanish into the golden magnificence of the
Uspensky. The ceremony seemed to last for hours. Bursts of singing emanated to us without, while in a cloud of incense Nicolas knelt before the jewelled sanctuary, following the rites which
owed their origin to the ancient Byzantine Empire.

Noon had passed when the Emperor and Empress came out
of the Cathedral with great diamond crowns on their heads.
Amid the pealing of bells a mighty shout arose from the waiting city. Carrying sceptres and weighted by their robes the mon-
archs walked slowly across the wide courtyard to the Kremlin
Palace. The sun blazed down, and the long procession following
them seemed to turn into a molten river of gold cloth and precious stones. Looking towards the Palace I saw two small figures
ascend the ancient Red Steps, but despite their gorgeous symbolic
apparel and regal bearing they walked as if bearing heavy bur-
dens as well as crowns. At the top of the steps they turned to bow
many times and the shouting grew in intensity. I could not take
my eyes from Nicolas, Emperor of All the Russias, at whose feet
the love of a vast nation seemed to surge.

Our duties done by late afternoon, we pages were allowed to wander about the town. Towards dusk I saw a group of frenzied people rushing along, a strange sound coming from their throats, a kind of stifled moan of misery and terror; then a huge peasant bumped against me, his face white and set, his great hands clasped as if beseeching God as he ran. A flood of hysterical people seemed to be flowing past us and we ran on feverishly hoping for excitement. Then we met the carts, looking quite ordinary from a distance, just carts covered with tarpaulins, but drawing near we saw they carried loads of human bodies with stiffened arms and legs protruding grotesquely. Then came more carts, some without covers, and we ran on in the direction of the Khodinski Fields from which they came. With the incredible callousness of youth we stared at bleeding heaps of peasants. I saw a child, its little dead face distorted with pain, still clinging to what had been a woman. We enquired of distressed passers-by what had happened, but they pushed us away and we were too weary to be really curious.

The incredible tragedy of the Khodinski Fields seems like an evil portent. The authorities had arranged for thousands of souvenir Coronation mugs attractively stamped with the Imperial Monogram to be given away on the outskirts of Moscow. Large wedge-shaped structures were built with narrow openings at which the mugs could be slowly and methodically dealt out. The overwhelming crowds, surpassing prevision, pushed too eagerly into the V-shaped stands and became jammed. Unaware of this, the back ranks drove greedily forward, pressing heavily on those caught against the bottle-necked barriers. The few who got through the turnstiles might be compared to water dropping slowly from a large cistern. Pandemonium broke loose when those crushed against the stands fell and were trampled under-foot as the pressure increased. Screams filled the air. Women and children fainted and died with desperate cries stifled in their throats. In an hour two thousand were crushed and stamped to death.

The Emperor and Empress, hardly out of their Coronation robes, were greeted with this terrible news. Their reign had begun as it was to end, in ghastly suffering which they, kindly, well-meaning people, were powerless to avert. After a sleepless night they had to drive through the festooned city and, though loudly acclaimed, their faces showed only forced, joyless smiles.

Enquiries were made. Who was responsible for the wedge-shaped stands with small outlets? Each official blamed another. The Emperor gave large sums of money to the bereaved and injured, but the dead do not come back to life, and the ever-superstitious Russians were filled with gloomy forebodings. The double eagle seemed to have spread black wings of evil omen over this reign which had hardly begun.

That night Mother came to see me in bed. She still wore her tiara and regulation court dress with red velvet sleeves. Her black hair sparkled with diamonds.

"My own," she said, using my special Russian pet name. "Do not forget this day."

CHAPTER 2

Of Curl-papers & Mrs Potter—
Of the Charm of My Mother
& the Gaiety of My Father—
Of Our Journey to Odessa

I HAVE NOT FORGOTTEN. In London one often sees Khodinski mugs standing on a mantel or table of knick-knacks. To me they never fail to bring back every detail of that far-off, incredible day in the white city of Moscow. Is it possible? I wonder. Could I have really been that little boy in the thronged Kremlin and was it really I who years later would find only a heap of ashes in the dark Siberian forest and count the bayonet-holes in that blood-stained Ekaterinburg cellar? Then from the depths of one's mind pour many pictures, hazy and vivid by turn, and one goes back through the unproportioned memories of very young days, to a world that hate and passion have swept away.

I suppose I must have been a fairly attractive child, for innumerable relations doted on me. Born in the Officers' Quarters of the Chevalier Guards Barracks in Petrograd, I had a delightful if brief career, being constantly lifted onto the crackling silk knees of Mother's friends, patted, stroked and applauded. Officers in white uniforms enriched with gold epaulettes would stand me on the dinner-table, begging that I should relate my dreams, and for the first few years all my remarks seemed to have a singular success. But too soon the days passed and all that changed. Taken out of my white lace dress, I was clad in ordinary sailor suits like my two elder brothers. Admiration stopped and lessons began.

All through these early years rustled one dominating personality without which no Petersburg family was complete, Mrs Potter, the tremendous, indispensable, invulnerable English Nanny.

She had been lured from her beloved country to look after the children of Alexander II, the grandeur of this position atoning for dreadful Russian tea. Owing to a broken leg she came to us, and soon held a position of unique importance in the household, even Father regarding her with wholesome respect. And to show her independence, her scorn for everything not English, Emma Potter lived twenty-five years in Russia without learning to speak our "barbaric" tongue.

We children spoke English before Russian and our infant imaginations were fed with tales of that far, wonderful country. We knew more about Robin Hood than about Stenka Rasin, and tales of West Drayton, where Mrs Potter's children lived, made Moscow seem dull. The Russian aristocracy was the most cosmopolitan in the world. We thought in Russian, spoke French and English between ourselves and used German for technical discussions.

Mrs Potter's limp warned us who approached when we were up to mischief, but though unable to give chase she carried a light whip hidden in her voluminous skirts and occasionally we got a flick. She was, of course, a snob, the best type of traditional English snob, the backbone of an Empire. She could not help being impressed by the magnificence of Imperial Russia. Court receptions, decorations, and titles gave her a secret joy, but when anything went wrong she moaned for England, and would hum "Britannia rules the Waves," mournfully and slightly off-key, in true British fashion. I was always puzzled as to who wanted to turn the great powerful Britons into slaves. Even her respect for the Tzar was increased by the fact that he was so nearly related to the Family at Windsor.

Yet Nana was tied to Russia by her love for us, and every few years, when she did go off to visit her family, she forgot the horrors of exile and invariably departed in tears. After each holiday she returned with new tales, and when her son got a job on the railway we had cake for tea instead of lettuce and milk!

Extraordinary things were done to children in those days. For instance, we boys had to sleep in knobbly curl-papers till a few years before we started military training! Then from being befrilled, beribboned dolls we were turned over to French governesses and German tutors, and sternly prepared for an officer's life.

One day when I was about five, Mama came into the nursery in her silk rustling skirts and took me on her knee:

"Pavlic, how would you like to be a page at a wedding? Would you be a good little boy?"

"Yes, yes, of course." A wedding savoured of excitement and cake. Voluble promises poured forth.

Mother's cousin Princess Aurora Demidoff was to marry Prince Arseni Karageorgievitch, a Serb attached to the Chevalier Guards Regiment.

At rehearsals I conducted myself well, and on the exciting day allowed Mrs Potter to put on my new suit, and fuss and curl for hours.

"My cherub, don't forget there will be royalties watching." At last "looking my best," with a halo of tight corkscrew curls I drove off with my parents to the regimental church of the Chevalier Guards.

Mama instructed me carefully all the way, until I imagined myself the central figure in the coming ceremony.

How crowded it was in the church! The air seemed thick with incense and voices, and my ears hummed with instructions. At last the procession was ready, and I walked proudly up the aisle carrying the sacred ikon in front of the wedding pair.

Afterwards I was kissed, popped into the bridal carriage and drove off with Aunt Aurora in her shimmering bridal dress and her husband in his white Chevalier Guards uniform. Of the reception I recall only plates of strawberries and being given a gold watch, whose poor insides soon exploded from overwinding.

After the murder of King Obroenovitch of Serbia, Prince Arseni's brother became King, and the son of that handsome pair before whom I carried the ikon is now Prince Paul, Regent of Yugoslavia.

Then Father left the Army and we went to Odessa to stay with Mother's grandfather, Count Alexander Strogonoff. For three days we travelled southwards over the Russian plains—Papa, Mama and four squawking children with a bevy of attendants. Mrs Potter flounced and slapped, while Father admonished us in gruff Russian and Mother, as always, pleaded in English. His Cossack valet bullied a herd of porters; her French maid had "migraine" and sniffed smelling-salts. When plaiting Mother's hair at night she had to back out of the compartment and down the corridor before she could finish.

Mrs Potter tried to keep us quiet by reading *David Copperfield*, whose depressing adventures cast a shroud of gloom over us all. At length she gave up and stared disapprovingly out at the wild plains and vast forests through which we passed. In England there were no three-day journeys!

My father, Captain Paul Rodzianko, was an officer of the type only that fantastic age could produce. He was chivalrous, licentious, fearless, senseless and artistic all at the same time. His family had left the Ukraine and joined the Russian court after the death of Ivan Skoropadsky, the last independent Hetman of the Ukraine in 1722. From then on the Hetman was but an honorary title till in 1756 Catherine the Great incorporated the Ukraine in the Russian Empire.

Father entered the Chevalier Guards as his father and grandfather had before him, and became a good shot and first-class horseman. Any English soldier who dabbled with the arts would be dubbed a "queer fellow" and regarded with suspicion. But in Russia artistic capacities in officers were the rule rather than the exception. Poetry, painting and science were discussed in the mess as frequently as women, and most officers were very musical. My father went through a phase of landscape painting and his watercolours hung in the lesser-used bathrooms of our various houses, but his real passion was music. He knew many operas by heart and himself composed a number of songs and marches (among them a family march, "Cassez Tout," with no words but plenty of action, which was played whenever he entered a restaurant). Unfortunately he was well aware of his own charm and had a gay life, but music remained the passion of his heart. Many men intend to "live for the day" and not let possible consequences trouble them, but Father was among the few who put this philosophy into practice. Whatever he wanted to do he did, right away without any worry. He dared anything. He did not wait for things to come to him, what he wanted out of life he damn well took.

Tall, slim and handsome with the most disarming smile in his blue eyes—such was Father's appearance as he strolled his merry, wilful way. There were other such personalities in that age, glamorous, eccentric, useless except in the sphere they were bred in. In the struggle of modern mechanical life they simply could not exist.

It was at a court ball that Captain Rodzianko first met our mother, Princess Marie Galitzine, daughter of Prince Paul Galitzine and Countess Natalie Strogonoff, heiress of the famous Siberian fortune.

Having been strictly brought up by a series of French, English and German governesses, Mother came out at the age of eighteen and was made lady-in-waiting to the Empress Marie.

She was tall and dark with huge smouldering eyes and a dynamic personality. Her heavy black hair was the longest I have ever seen, actually touching the floor when she stood. As a schoolgirl she went to France with her aunt the Grand Duchess Marie Nicolaevna. Mother's hair then hung in long plaits, and as she walked along the promenade at Nice two men started whispering behind her. One of them suddenly gave the plaits a sharp tug. Mother screamed with pain and her aunt whirled furiously.

"Sorry," drawled an English voice, "I had a bet it wasn't real."

"Quelle impertinence," gasped the Grand Duchess, and marched her unfortunate niece on.

When Mother plunged from the school-room to court life her vivacious intellect and energy made her swiftly popular. She could be equally witty in four languages and many officers fell in love with her. When she met Father he was already famous for wild pranks and success with the ladies. She looked at his aquiline profile, danced a mazurka and made up her lightning mind.

Officers of the Chevalier Guards had special living quarters in Petrograd and we children were born in barracks. Rodzianko boys were entered at birth for the famous military school, the "Corps des Pages." The Empress Marie (sister of Queen Alexandra) was Hon. Chief of Father's regiment, and he commanded Her Majesty's squadron until at last his peculiar sense of humour brought him trouble. No one ever knew what he would be up to next. One evening he rode upstairs to the officers' mess on his charger. When Kaiser Wilhelm II visited Petrograd the Chevalier Guards gave him an official dinner, and Father started to play the fool. A great deal of wine flowed, and when at the end of dinner the regimental singers entered he persuaded His Majesty to sit on a soldier's coat on the floor. After their performance the singers lifted the Kaiser high in the air and swung him about, singing mightily. But Alexander III, very strict and austere, who discouraged revelry among officers, heard of this indecorous behaviour and disapproved strongly.

Several months later another incident proved the last straw. At that time a great deal was drunk at regimental dinners in all countries, and Father being naturally wild did not improve with alcohol. The soldiers adored him and he was always arranging amusements for them, but at length he went too far. One night amidst the applause of fellow officers he summoned his men:

"Little brothers," he announced, "I am going to give you all a treat at my expense."

The whole sleepy squadron was ordered to proceed as his guests to a certain famous gay establishment. Thinking it a fine joke, the soldiers fell in and obeyed the order, "Quick march," with zest. Off they tramped, their boots crunching the stiff snow, their broad grins veiled by darkness.

Petrograd on a winter night is uncannily still, a city under a pall of snow, lifeless as the steppes. The crack of a twig echoes like a rifle-shot. Suddenly this silence is broken by the sound of cymbals, drums, whistles and trumpets, a blast of military music grows louder and louder, shattering the cold air.

Through the deserted streets appears my father marching at the head of his squadron with the band in full swing; blood-stirring soldiers' songs awaken citizens, curtains are pulled and startled faces peer out.

The squadron marches on in perfect order, leaving consternation in its wake. As always the *baunchuk*, a stick hung with bells and ribbons presented by ladies of the squadron, was carried in front and clanged in time. Although inwardly bursting with laughter, the men maintained complete discipline until reaching their destination on the outskirts of Petrograd:

"Halt!" shouted my father: and then "Dismiss!"

His guests were well attended to with champagne and other attractions. Towards dawn the squadron was reformed and marched back to barracks with ranks less rigidly formed as the band played strange harmonies, the men still singing, but not quite so loudly.

Next day Father, hazy and subdued, appeared before his commanding officer.

"My dear Paul," said the old General, "the whole Army knows what you did last night. Even you cannot get away with this."

So with his usual careless grace Father resigned from the Army and continued his eccentric career in the country. Our Mother arranged everything to amuse him, and went on bearing children and gazing at him with great, dark adoring eyes. But Father soon regretted his military life. Court balls and the narrow if cultured "society" of Petrograd could not atone for the loss of his beloved squadron.

To distract him we all went off to stay with Mother's grandfather in Odessa.

On arriving at the ancient port we were bustled to a hotel to be washed, brushed and clad in clean sailor suits. Then we drove in open carriages to the Strogonoff house.

We stopped in front of the grey stone mansion overlooking the Black Sea. Several enormous footmen hurried to meet us dressed

in livery and covered with medals, for Great-grandfather had military tastes and his servants were ex-soldiers.

The old man waited for us in his study where he sat in a high-
backed velvet chair. He rose to meet us, over six feet in spite of his
ninety years, with a white beard and piercing blue eyes. Mamma
kissed him. Father clicked heels and bowed and everyone spoke
at the same time in French, which at that time was used for light
conversation. In identical sailor suits the children went up to kiss
his hand in turn.

I was at the stage when I still wore my white lace dress after
tea, and in this always successful attire I gave an acrobatic or theatrical performance every evening on the mat in front of the fire.
Great-grandfather took me on his knee and related the romantic
story of the acquisition of his family possessions, which were, in
fact, a reward for discovering Siberia!

In the sixteenth century Ivan the Terrible induced one of his
most troublesome Cossack warriors, Yermak, to set off and conquer Siberia. Strogonoff, a Moscow merchant, grown tired of
trading life, went with him to explore the unknown lands beyond the Urals. The handful of brave fighters struggled across the
wilderness of mountains, rivers, swamps and forests, skirmishing
constantly with ferocious Mongolian tribes. During the summer
months the men penetrated deep into the interior, hunting game.
All winter they camped in the snow.

After several years, in 1581, they returned to Moscow bringing back sledges of furs and roughly hacked precious stones to lay
before the Tzar. Ivan united the great new land to Russia, and to
Strogonoff he gave large territories that descended from father to
son until they reached my great-grandfather.

Every day during that summer at Odessa I walked along the
seashore with the old man and he talked of a past he remembered
distinctly. Born soon after the French Revolution he had grown
up during the Napoleonic invasion, in the Russia of Tolstoy's *War
and Peace*. At an extremely early age he became A.D.C. to Alexander I and went to Paris with the Tzar, after Waterloo.

"I never saw Napoleon," he said, "but I saw his city just after he had left it—the Paris of 1815 lost, deserted, bereft of its Eagle, the streets full of foreign flags and uniforms. It was Russia that broke him."

No one has yet solved the mystery of Alexander I. Nothing has yet proved or disproved that he helped plan the murder of his father, lunatic Paul I, or that he himself really died at Taranrog. It was a strange story. The brilliant, handsome Alexander guided Russia through the days of Napoleon, took the stage at the Congress of Vienna and built up the Holy Alliance, and then, so many people said, arranged a mock death and retired to end his days in a hut in Siberia. As Feodor Kusmitch he lived till 1864, alone, meditating, refusing to see anyone.

My great-grandfather, who was on duty by the body *en route* as A.D.C., must have known, but he denied the story. The papers he left on the subject he asked Father to burn. Father died far from us all without telling.

When the militaristic Nicolas I came to the throne Great-grandfather remained the Emperor's A.D.C. and also became his political adviser. After the difficult days of 1825 and the famous December Revolt, inspired by the nobility who objected to Byzantine autocracy, Strogonoff took a strong stand about the numerous Jewish pogroms and told the Emperor frankly they must be stopped by stern measures. The Russians' in-bred loathing and mistrust of the Jews could not be stamped out, but Strogonoff argued, "Although the Jews ask for trouble, pogroms are against the basic laws of Christianity, and the Russians are a Christian people." The Tzar took Strogonoff's advice and gradually pogroms were suppressed. But the hate remained, and when the time came for the downfall of Imperial Russia, the Jews did not forget.

When Nicolas I died his brother Alexander II ascended the throne, and Strogonoff still remained the Tzar's adviser. A very wise man, he really understood Russia, and made a link between Emperor and people which was to be sorely needed in the next century and which no man filled.

Then the drawing-rooms of Petrograd began to gossip, and a scandal of the most unexpected kind shook the poor Count.

His only son Gregory and the Grand Duchess Marie Nicolaevna, daughter of Nicolas I, fell in love. Everything was done to separate them, but of no avail. The Emperor and Empress decided to give in, and the Empress sent for old Strogonoff.

"My husband and I," she explained, "are convinced this is a deep and serious love, and we are willing to give our consent to the marriage. Don't be so hard on your son. Let the young people be happy."

"Madame," replied Great-grandfather, "if it is an order I will give my consent, for I have to obey my sovereign's orders, but otherwise never."

"Oh, ne faites pas tant de tragique," cried the Empress.

But the old man remained obdurate. Until the Emperor himself commanded him he would not consent.

The marriage took place.

"I'd rather he'd chosen a cook," was the old Count's only remark. "Strogonoffs are born to *serve* Russia and the house of Romanoff, not to marry their Grand Duchesses."

Whereupon he left Petrograd for ever and settled in Odessa. Nothing could lure him back. He was made Governor of the Province and for thirty years turned his energies to sound administration.

Although Strogonoff never got over the *mésalliance* the years tempered his disgust. Contrary to his expectations the marriage turned out very happily, and the couple often came to see him. Whenever members of the royal family visited Odessa they stayed with old Strogonoff, so that in the end he held quite a little court of his own in the plain grey house by the Black Sea.

CHAPTER 3

Life in Petrograd—Much Learning
& the Enchantments of the Ukraine

HAVING SERVED RUSSIA under five Tzars our great-grandfather died at the age of nearly a hundred, leaving the Strogonoff fortune divided between his two grand-daughters, Helen, the only child of Gregory and the Grand Duchess, and my mother.

In Russia a "fortune" did not generally mean invested capital, it meant land. Our money came from the earth, our incomes depended on the harvests, for they were derived from the sale of corn and wheat as well as from the selling of timber from endless tracts of forests. In the extraordinary financial world of the Russian aristocracy "money" meant nothing. We never knew what our yearly income was, never bothered to find out. Most estates were run by efficient German agents and everything lay in their hands. They dealt with all business, wrote us long letters about sales and matters we could not understand and reproved extravagant members of the family. My parents worked hard to improve their estates, knew the peasants, built hospitals and railways, helped the poor and sick. But they were incapable of taking charge from the financial point of view. Poor, conscientious, hard-working German agents, their distressed faces were to be seen in every big house. I suppose they regarded us as a race apart, as inexplicable cases of intelligent people with whom one could discuss anything but finance. I am afraid our agent was among the most frantic, for though Mother would sit through long solemn conferences she never really understood anything, and Father began to squander more recklessly than ever.

Even the children cannot help knowing what is going on, for the noise of revels keeps us awake at night. Until dawn the house resounds with the noise of trumpets, drums and guitars. We creep from our beds to watch the merriment in the hall downstairs; gypsies singing and dancing in their brilliant clothes, the women twist and turn with flashing smiles, and beat time with their slim brown hands, while men leap in the air performing traditional Cossack steps with incredible speed and skill. Then comes a moment's silence, the balalaikas begin and strange wild voices are raised in song. Next morning we cannot do our lessons, for our ears still ring with savage, sorrowful tunes.

Mother inherited some of the fabulous Strogonoff jewels, mostly huge emeralds from Siberia. Next to the Imperial family the Yousoupoffs and Strogonoffs had the most beautiful collections in Russia. The Empress Marie once laughingly asked Mother, "Do not wear emeralds the same night as I do. Yours make mine look pale."

Soon after this, Father rejoined the Army in the Caucasus. For two years he commanded a Cossack regiment, and when he finally retired as a Colonel he was made Equerry at court. For years our poor Mother was chaffed over an incident at a court ball when one of her petticoats fell off. The Grand Duke Nicolas picked it up and put it in his helmet. Mother sighed with relief and thought no one else would notice, when suddenly he pulled it out, waved it over his head and presented it to her with a flourish. It was no good pretending it did not belong to her, for her blushes betrayed all to the laughing court.

As years rolled by, the curls Mrs Potter had wetted and twisted were shaven off and only a stiff, straight, manly crop of bristles remained standing upright on top of my head.

Like all Russian children of our class we had to submit to hours of work under French and German tutors, poor exiles caught in the vastest, most lonely country in the world. Like Ireland, Russia had an odd effect on foreigners. A generation on Irish soil can turn the most stolid English family into a tribe of impecunious, poetical eccentrics. Those who lived many years in Russia found contact with their own lands somehow severed. They never really fitted into Russian life, yet Russia held them, the restless spirit of the plains destroyed their peace and their own countries seemed tame and dull when they returned.

Our tutor, Carl Ivanovitch Tornius, was a typical, kind-hearted, fat-necked Teuton whose loud "Kinder Aufstehen Sie" woke us every morning as he pattered in in huge slippers and voluminous dressing-gown. He had less success than Mrs Potter, for now we knew that hours of study awaited us. Herr Tornius was *gewissenhaft* to a degree and took his duties very seriously. It worried him that we never acquired the mentality of good German boys of the type that committed suicide after failing in exams.

Although we had to study hard with the daily tutors who came for various subjects, we managed to get a lot of fun. During the winter in Petrograd we skated every day with many other children on the rink of the flooded grounds of the Taurida Palace. A wooden tower with an ice shoot had been built at each end of the lake and we used them as toboggan runs. Marvellous, invigorating afternoons, the dry frosty atmosphere made one's blood warm. I worked hard at figure skating and accomplished the feat of skating down the ice shoots backwards on one leg. This tricky performance was reserved for large and appreciative audiences. One day, having collected a crowd of small girls, I blissfully started to show off. To excited gasps I climbed the shoot and came sailing down, one leg in the air. I was smiling, when suddenly my head hit the ice. Frightened governesses carried me off unconscious, and it was weeks before I again shouted "Watch me skate."

One of the few women to go down these shoots was the beautiful Lady Randolph Churchill when she came to Petrograd with her husband.

Unlike English children of this period, who sat through hours of gloomy preaching, we looked forward to church on Sunday. The Byzantine splendour of Russian churches and the glorious singing gave us a vigorous idea of religion; above all, one associated God with power, beauty and harmony. Pantomimes were tawdry in comparison. The soulful madonnas of the Roman church, the gentle cherubic holy children of Raphael never entered our imagination. The God of our childhood was God the Father—superhuman, golden, shining. His voice, the voice of thunder, echoed in the deep soul-stirring choruses, bass voices blending velvet and steel, that only Russia can breed. As a rule we went to the Strogonoff Church in the Mokhovaia, where the singing of the carefully chosen voices was supreme.

Sunday afternoons were often spent in the Winter Palace playing with our cousins, the sons of Prince Troubetskoy, Grand Chamberlain of the Emperor. One of these boys, Peter, subsequently married my sister. It was fun exploring the Palace, running through enormous unused rooms and sliding down the slippery corridors. Long passages led to the Hermitage where there was a life-sized figure of Peter the Great. Ingeniously moved by a mechanical device this figure could stand up and bow, but unfortunately a lady had fainted with shock at the sight and it was not allowed to work.

Sometimes we drove out to Marino where my uncle, Prince Paul Galitzine, owned a beautiful eighteenth-century palace built by the Italian Rastrelli. Thrilling with excitement, we were occasionally taken to the great library where false bookcases pulled back and revealed a cupboard full of old French uniforms and other belongings captured by a Strogonoff who attacked Davoust during the retreat. Among other things was the case for Davoust's Field-Marshal's baton, which we handled with awe. The baton itself had been hung over Koutousoff's grave, but we were so often told the story of that empty box that it impressed us more than any object. An empty box and dead men's uniforms hanging in a secret cupboard! What could be more sinister? Our vivid imaginations turned historical facts into ghost stories, terrible as they were vague. Rumour spread among us that the library was haunted, and Uncle Paul often laughed when he saw us scuttling past it in the dark.

My only sister came out at about this time. Terrific excitement reigned in our house when she was being dressed for balls, and we peeped with awe at her gorgeous white dresses. A few months after being presented, she was elected Maid of Honour. The diamond *chiffre* of the two Empresses, Marie and Alexandra, was sent with its blue ribbon by special courier. Everyone fluttered with delight, and of course Father opened a number of bottles of champagne.

When spring came and the snow melted from the streets, we started working with additional vigour, for every May came the Public Examinations. An unnatural silence reigned in the schoolroom, and we crept gloomily about with books in every pocket.

The heat came swiftly, and once examinations were over we all left the city for one of Mother's country estates near Vitebsk, or a lovely old place called the "Wolf's Den" in the Ukraine, or to Nicolaevna near Voronege.

How good it was after months of hard study in Petrograd to get back to the wild black earth. No life has ever been as natural and attractive as the country life of Russia, and June in the Ukraine, the most fertile country of Europe, is a miracle.

As we approached "home" I looked out at the brilliant green meadows, glistening corn-fields and tracts of untouched forest and plains covered with flowers. Villages of whitewashed cottages with thatched roofs were baking under the sun, and gaily attired peasants working in the fields around. The orchards had lost their blossom by the time we arrived, but were soon heavy with fruit, and fields of watermelons lay at the disposal of thirsty travellers. It was a Ukrainian custom to plant water-melons at the roadside so that strangers could refresh themselves. The peasants were all prosperous and well dressed—how could they be otherwise in such a country? Every man owned his plot of land, his cattle, poultry, pigs and often a horse. Above all, he owned his free soul. There had never been serfs or oppression among this tall, strong, Ukrainian agricultural-military people. "A noble" was one who proved himself so. They held out longer than any other part of Russia against the communist system, which they have never yet learnt to understand. When the Commissar takes away the Ukrainian's plot of land and his cattle and tries to make him a slave on a collective farm, he takes away also his individuality and the pride he has inherited from generations of fighting farmers.

The Ukrainian countryside is as different from north Russia as California is from the Middle West. It is a warm luxuriant land and its Cossack people are unlike the Russians of the north, who have mixed with the Mongols. Many of the best men in the Russian Army were Ukrainians. The men were as famous for their physique and courage as the women for their beauty.

When our train entered the station several troikas were waiting (a troika is a sledge or carriage drawn by three horses, the centre horse trots while the side ones gallop).

Our parents' troika was always drawn by three greys. The rest of us jumped into the other carriages with their well-marked horses and off the procession started at great speed. A mounted escort from the estate galloped around us and we knew the holidays had really begun.

Mrs Potter disapproved of troikas, which went at a great pace. She followed sedately in a closed carriage, unimpressed and unamused by the shouting guard.

At the village gate a crowd of peasants met us with the traditional welcome offering of bread and salt. The "Starosta," a primitive head-man, elected for the administrative and policing purposes of the village, came to meet us. In his high boots, wide trousers, embroidered shirt and sheepskin hat he stepped forward and presented the black dome-shaped loaf and cup of salt on a wooden tray. We all tasted. Bells pealed as we drove on, and the priest in his tall hat was waiting on the doorstep of our house to bless us.

Gifts and money were always bestowed on the occasion of the bread-and-salt ritual, so the peasants never failed to rush out whenever a member of the family passed the village. This practice got so trying that one day I induced the coachman to let me squeeze a pig into the closed carriage and drive to the village.

As he approached, a crowd of clamouring children precipitated themselves into the roadway with outstretched hands. The carriage stopped and with a furious squeal the face of my pig appeared at the window. The whole village grinned for several days.

Our first day at the Wolf's Den was the best of the year. Having torn through the rambling house, we descended to the kitchen to greet our friend the cook and eat a few dozen home-made cakes.

While nurses gloomily unpacked, we children set out to explore the park and gardens and examine our pets. One could roam for hours through the grounds, and beyond lay thousands of miles of orchards, golden fields, dark forests and tracts of untouched country.

Far back among my earliest memories, when I must have been a very little boy, I can recall a hot afternoon and a large ploughed field that seems far from home (but everything seemed farther and bigger in those days!). I must be about five, and have gone out alone to explore. I come upon a stationary plough drawn by two oxen, cross and much teased by flies. All the oxen I have previously met have been charming and friendly. Up I waddle to pat the big white haunch. Ow! the end of the world! What a kick! Catching me where the solar plexus would some day develop, the ox's hoof sent me flying into a bush several feet away. The pain, the terror! My mouth opens to howl but no sound comes. I can't breathe, I can't cry. Silent, salt tears course down a small purple face. Hateful oxen, never again will I trust your kindly eyes! Gasping, choking, I crawl pitifully homewards, straight to the nursery, straight to Mrs Potter. Still unable to breathe (it seems) I clutch her skirts, splutter a terrible incomprehensible story, am soothed, given hiccough medicine and wait for the power of weeping to return.

What a curious jumbled box one's memory is, some fragments so clear, others forgotten. Still I can smell the earth that warm afternoon and feel the prick of the bushes! It gives me a pain in the diaphragm to write this little story that happened half a century ago!

Then we grew older. When not riding or swimming we stuffed ourselves with peaches and water-melons in the orchard. Mrs Pot-

ter noticing diminished appetites took to lying in wait for us, but
now we could run away laughing, with bulging pockets, knowing
our long legs could keep us out of reach.

There were about a hundred horses in the stables and a large
retinue of grooms, mostly ex-soldiers of my Father's regiment.
None who served in the Chevalier Guards and asked for em-
ployment was ever turned away. Roaring with laughter, an ex-
Sergeant-Major used to tell me of Father's numerous exploits in
the Army.

We loved these old soldiers who drilled us and were drilled in
turn as soon as we learnt the words of command. They adored
and spoilt us in a way Mrs Potter quivered to see. At the age
of ten I formed a private squadron of picked men and proudly
rode at their head. During long trotting expeditions through the
woods I suffered agonizing stitches but dared not stop. Then we
would detect some peasant and, to his bewilderment, charge.
Riding home in the twilight when the heavy gold sun was slipping behind the horizon and the woods mysterious with shadows,
I would give the signal for music and fifteen lusty voices would
ring forth in the Cossack marching songs their fathers had fought
and died to. No music can be so beautiful and yet so war-like.

Those voices are in my heart still.

On Sunday we walked to church, a red-and-white wooden
church with a blue cupola and five golden crosses. Every Saturday
the peasants had steam baths and prepared for Sunday as a festival. It was a gorgeous sight as they flocked into church in their
bright clothes. The girls wore the lovely Ukrainian flowered head-
dress and brilliant blouses and skirts and highly coloured boots.
The men had wide Cossack trousers, leather boots and shirts
embroidered in every colour by their best girls. Many came from
villages ten miles away, and all country churches had a big space
in which to keep the horses and little carriages during the service.

Inside, the church was painted gold and white with strange old
wooden ikons in front of the altar. Masses of field flowers were
placed before the ikons and many candles burned. Our family
had a sort of box to stand in, and if a lady felt faint a chair would

be fetched with much clatter and commotion. The congregation stood or knelt on a stone floor, bowing low in prayer. They were, I suppose, the richest, healthiest, handsomest peasantry in the world. The fertility of the good earth made overwork and under-feeding unknown. They all lived well, and came to church not to escape from hard materialism but to rejoice and to show off their lovely apparel. How different from the little chapels of Ireland, where, in spite of the poetry in them, the peasants come to mass work-worn and humble! There was of course no organ, only mag-nificent singing.

In the choir of strong natural voices were splendid basses. The musical talent of the peasants amazed foreigners. Under a good conductor they sang Tchaikovsky's most complicated Masses to perfection.

After service the multi-coloured crowd streamed out of church in all directions, laughing, talking and flirting. They were a light-hearted people, less introspective and passive than the northern Russian peasants.

The priest and his wife usually lunched with us on Sundays. In Russia a priest can marry only once, so they chose healthy buxom lasses! Our priest was very good-looking, his fine features, long hair and beard making him so Christ-like that in very early days I thought he *was* the Galilean.

His charm and simplicity made him a welcome visitor in our house. It was the simplicity of an intelligent man accustomed to talking to peasants in the clear, direct way they understand. He worked hard for the old and sick and troubled, and Mother used to have long discussions with him about the new hospitals she was building on her estates. In spite of his gentleness, the father had plenty of courage and would tackle any of his flock who were drunkards or misbehaved. Vodka did infinite harm to the peas-ants; they never learned temperance and a great hulking man drunk often committed crimes unknowingly.

One Sunday a very poor priest from a neighbouring village drove over in his cart to lunch. To our delight he drank out of the finger-bowl and we all followed suit.

When our Father went away we devised new entertainments. The grooms loved to join in. I invented a "follow-the-leader." All horse-driven carriages were ordered out, with a groom on the back of each horse for "suppling exercises." They lined up one behind the other, troikas, traps, dogcarts and landaus. I started off in front, with the caravan twisting and turning through the grounds after me. One day the last cart upset near the house. It contained our milk supply and foaming cans crashed in all directions. That was the last time I impressed the countryside with the "caterpillar of death."

But Father had his own little diversions.

"Why have we no lake in front of the house?" he asked one hot day.

"There is no water, sir," answered the agent.

"La belle affaire . . . Send for an engineer."

Someone had heard of an English well expert staying about a hundred miles away. That distance meant nothing in the Ukraine and he was promptly summoned.

"I want a lake," explained Father, pointing to the shady lawn. The Englishman looked dazed but offered to do his best. He was installed in the best bedroom and treated like a genius. After much plotting and planning he proceeded to drill a deep artesian well to catch a source of water. Then the whole village was employed in digging out the bed of the lake. Soon Mother complained the view had been spoilt by great heaps of earth, and the cook was exhausted trying to prepare refreshments for the workers.

Eventually the digging was completed, and pumps set to work to fill the lake. The result seemed superbly successful. Father was delighted and the engineer went off hurriedly with a fat cheque in his pocket. But Father's lake did not last long. When the pumps stopped, the water disappeared overnight.

"The engineer is a scoundrel, he cheated me," roared Father, "but I will have a lake."

A bed of clay was laid down. The pumps started work again and the water held! But in the summer heat the clay shores cracked and the water seeped away. Still it was not too bad, until my parents went away for a few days and I took Father's pet stag for a bathe in the lake. He enjoyed the dip, but his sharp hooves dug deep holes in the clay and out ran more water. The lake grew daily more hideous, till at last it had to be filled in.

Among the many relations who visited us was Father's brother, Michael Rodzianko, who was later head of the Duma when the Revolution broke out. Uncle Mischa was enormous, his deep voice and physical strength filled us with admiration and awe. He left the Chevalier Guards to look after his estates in the Ukraine.

One summer we went to stay with him. He was a Liberal, and took great personal interest in his property and the peasants. One day we were walking in the fields watching the harvest being gathered. The workers' food (always given by the employer) was being prepared in a large cauldron. Uncle had heard complaints against the lazy cook and went up, as he often did, to taste the thick borsh.

"Not good enough," he said to the fat fellow in charge of the cooking. The fat fellow answered impudently and a man called out the food was rotten. To our amusement Uncle suddenly lifted the huge cauldron, emptied it, put it on the cook's head and told him to make new stuff. We walked off to the delighted cheers of the men.

Unfortunately when Kerensky came into his office and asked him to quit Michael Rodzianko did not show the same resourcefulness, which, though it might seem crude in other countries, always appeals to Russians.

Summer in the Ukraine sped by, a glorious time, but as I grew older I preferred the autumn, for then wolf-hunting began. This sport requires as much skill and is a good deal more dangerous than fox-hunting, so at first I had to follow the hunt with the ladies in a carriage. This was mortifying, but better than seeing nothing. The huntsmen rode out in line. Each man had a borzoi dog, and they would slowly comb out a wood to start the wolf. Once in the open, the run was usually short and fast. If wolves were pillaging, the animal could be shot, but it was considered better sport to allow the *volkodav* (a large, rough-coated borzoi to which the soft European breed is not comparable) to attack the wolf and hold it at bay. The hunters galloped up and dismounted. One would wait for an opportunity to jump on the wolf's back and seize it by the ears. The dog was called off and a second hunter forced a wooden bit in the wolf's jaws and strapped his muzzle. Then the wolf could be brought back alive, which was the smart way of ending a chase. This form of sport compared, I suppose, to cubbing in England. As the frosts grew keener wolves became very fierce and dangerous through hunger. A man in our village was killed a few hundred yards from his house. Cows were always being eaten.

In winter the hunt proceeded on different lines and was much more exciting. Two or three hunters set off in a troika through the deep woods. Overhead glistened a dome of cold powdery stars and the trees and tree shadows stood blackly against the snow. For a time there was no sound but the crunch of the sledge. Then suddenly a squeal rang out. As a decoy a small pig had been taken in a sack, and when pinched his piteous voice rang out loudly. As the horses galloped on, one by one grey forms leapt out of the darker shadows and padded silently in the troika's wake. Ten, twenty, thirty, they pursued the sledge, leaping at the horses' heads. Wild with fear the animals plunged forward at break-neck pace, and the driver had to keep his head while the others shot at the ghostly silhouettes streaking across the snow. When a wolf fell, the hungry pack stopped to tear their brother to bits and the speed could be eased, but soon the phosphorescent eyes would close in on the sledge again.

Woe to the hunter whose horses might stumble and fall or to the man whom a sharp turning flung out of the sledge!

Because of the danger I was not allowed as a boy to take part in this chase, even when I volunteered for the rôle of squealing decoy. When older I loved it, as I never really cared for shooting birds or deer. As a rule the hunt continued till daybreak, when the black-and-white world became slowly grey and the wolves slunk away from the merry rising sun.

CHAPTER 4

The Corps des Pages

WE WERE SITTING at lunch in Petrograd one autumn day when a wide-eyed maid announced mother's great friend, General Baron A. Knorring. Having grave news he asked to be allowed to break in on the family meal. We looked up with surprise at the General's serious countenance.

"What on earth has happened?" asked Mother nervously.

"My dear," he kissed her hand, "the Emperor is dead."

Dead silence in the room.

The butler put down his tray and crossed himself. Feeling the need of an apt remark and being under the influence of a new French tutor, I piped out: "Le roi est mort, vive le roi!"

For the first time in her life Mother turned to me blazing with anger: "Leave the room, Paul, and do not return."

I retired perplexed and humiliated at the failure of this *à propos* remark. Up in the schoolroom I told Mrs Potter, who promptly burst into tears and rushed off to inform the housekeeper.

Within a few hours the news spread throughout the city and the general hush seemed to penetrate even to our nursery. Black flags hung from windows, church bells were silenced and our servants went about with downcast faces. The Little Father of Russia was dead.

Alexander III had died in the Crimea as a result of injuries to his liver received in a railway accident several years before, when the Imperial train was wrecked by Nihilists and many people killed. Curiously the Emperor and his family escaped with bruises except for this one internal injury which was to prove fatal. Alexander's embalmed body was brought to Petrograd to be laid to rest in the Cathedral of the Petropavlovsk Fortress, where all the Tzars had been buried since Peter the Great.

Stillness reigned in the city. Women wore mourning and the officers who visited us had their gold buttons, braid and helmets covered with black crepe. For several days crowds streamed along the banks of the Neva to pay their last respects to the Emperor, who lay in state in the Cathedral.

Our turn came. We were solemnly dressed in our best sailor suits, cautioned how to behave, and the whole family piled into a great landau and drove off to the fortress. Mother looked strange, her tall figure in black with decorations shining on her chest.

We always teased Mother for loving her decorations, till once, going to a parade, the police stopped us. Mother threw back her cloak, revealing her orders, and was allowed through the barrier with her brood marching after her.

The Emperor had been very handsome and death beautified his stern features. Never having seen a dead man, a slight fear came over me when told to kiss the cross on his breast, but coming near I saw the calm of his waxen face, and he looked just as a dead king should.

The Emperor's funeral took place on a cold frosty day. The streets were lined with soldiers. From the windows of the Strogonoff house in the Nevsky Prospect we watched them marching. A terrific cannonade broke the silence when the Emperor's body was interred, and troops presented arms throughout the city. It was bitterly cold for the troops and having watched them march off we returned to our firesides, little recking it was the last time a Tzar would be laid to rest in the ancient fortress.

Some weeks later the new Emperor married his *fiancée*, Princess Alix of Hesse-Darmstadt. The marriage took place quietly, but preparations soon began for the Coronation ceremonies which were to be held in the city of Moscow a year and a half later.

Meanwhile the time came for me to enter the famous military school, the Corps des Pages of His Majesty. The old rococo palace had been built for the Knights of Malta by Paul I. Their Catholic church still stood in the grounds and was used by boys from Poland and Catholic countries. A secret passage was supposed to have led to the Imperial Palace down which that madly cruel Tzar tried to escape from his murderers who choked him to death in 1801.

The building was painted deep red, and silhouetted against the frosty sky it had a peculiar beauty. Large gardens surrounded the college, green in summer, white with snow during the winter.

Having succeeded in the entry examinations, I shed my sailor suits and a wonderful new outfit appeared. I now wore long black trousers with a red stripe, had gold trimmings on my coat and a jaunty military cap perched over one eye. On the thrilling spring morning when I was driven to the Corps I felt myself a soldier for the first time.

Having entered the Corps one suddenly became grown-up and could go out unaccompanied. Of course the new boys fancied themselves tremendously and we would wander through the streets searching for officers to salute.

Only sons and grandsons of Generals or of officers killed in service were permitted to apply to the Corps des Pages, which was under the Tzar's personal supervision. In those days when the Army was the greatest career, the six hundred boys were considered the luckiest in Russia.

I already had one brother, Alex, in this military academy; the other, Vladimir, entered the Royal Naval College. Most of the Grand Dukes passed through the Corps des Pages, and among the foreigners I can remember King Alexander of Yugoslavia, the sons of the King of Siam and the son of the Emir of Bokhara.

As the Coronation approached we got restive with excitement, as all hoped to be selected to go to Moscow to attend someone during the ceremony.

After the Coronation my parents sent me travelling with a friend. It was the first time I had left Russia, and never before had I worn ordinary civilian clothes. Until the Corps des Pages we boys wore sailor suits, then only uniform, for in Russia pages and officers were never allowed to wear mufti, nor could soldiers smoke in the streets. It was one long, continuous parade.

I joined Sasha Ourousoff who was going to visit his father Prince Ourousoff, then Ambassador in Vienna. After a few weeks at the Embassy we travelled on to Paris and Italy. Ourousoff stayed in Vienna. I did the return journey alone.

I had to spend a night in Moscow, "White Stone City" of gay Oriental streets. In the Slave Bazaar Hotel I found a gypsy orchestra playing and made friends with the leader, who found me quite a connoisseur of Tzigane music owing to Father's training and they played on while I sipped sickly port in a haze of bilious sophistication.

But in truth I had been tremendously impressed by the countries that lay beyond the borders of our Empire, countries so different from our Russia, how different the years were bitterly to teach.

After a few weeks at the Wolf's Den we returned to Petrograd, and life continued its normal course in the Corps des Pages. We had excellent instruction from university professors and military experts, but according to modern standards the work was too severe for young boys. In winter I was up before dawn and drove to school in a sledge while the sun crept up and gilded the icebound Neva. We studied from eight until five with only a brief recreation for lunch. Day students such as myself then left the college with several hours' homework in prospect. This was seldom finished before ten or eleven at night, and at eight sharp next morning we had to be there for roll-call.

Marks were given daily and if any boy had less than 50% he was put under "arrest" and not allowed to leave school over the week-end. The mental strain was too severe, and although it gave the chance for an intellectual type to develop very highly, most boys burned their books in bonfires when the day came to depart.

It was however an interesting curriculum. We had the best professors and most brilliant lecturers on art, music, mathematics and politics. Any exceptional man of talent who visited Petrograd was asked to give us a lecture.

The Corps des Pages had a well-trained choir, the best singers and actors came to help us, and Petrograd had some very great artists in those days. Among the actors who came to explain the drama and coach us in plays which we produced at Christmas I remember the famous Davidoff.

We also had gymnastics and riding. Fencing began at fourteen with the best French and Italian masters. Fencing was really a very necessary and practical accomplishment as duels in later life were often fought with swords instead of pistols.

Being of an active disposition, I fretted for more exercise and less study. Boys often grew ill from overwork but I never had enough brain to get brain fever!

In spite of the amount of work I had enough energy to get into mischief and be severely punished. On one occasion I caught a mouse and let it loose in the skirts of a long-winded priest during Catechism, but unfortunately I was detected. We were subjected to military discipline right from the start. I was put under arrest and confined to a cell for several days. That evening the coachman returned home with a long face and a sad tale.

"Master Paul is under arrest."

After a lonesome night spent on a bench without a mattress, I began to explore my cell. In one corner stood a W.C. and I discovered the boards around could be loosened. Creeping down among the pipes, I carefully replaced the boards overhead and managed to escape. It was an icy early morning. Taking my coat from the empty cloak-room I strolled out to the nearest confectioner's. Restored by a hearty meal I wandered about, but my money was soon finished and towards evening I realized there was nothing to do but go home.

The butler opened the door and regarded me as one returned from the dead.

"Paul! . . ." gasped Mama.

"What the devil! . . . You young scoundrel!" Of course Father would be home!

"Back you go at once," buzzed a chorus of voices. Mrs Potter alone gazed pityingly over the banisters.

Before I had the chance to hide sweets or entertaining literature about my person, before indeed I realized anything, the carriage had been called and I found myself bundled back to school.

The authorities had been dumbfounded at my disappearance, but at length they discovered the loose boards and I spent a whole week in that dismal cell with the floor securely nailed down!

For a time I was subdued. Then a new geography master arrived and I could not resist assuming a stutter. For several weeks he took me for an unfortunate half-wit and I had a great success among the other boys. Then growing suspicious he asked General Danilowsky, General Inspector of the Corps des Pages, to attend class. A magic silence fell as soon as the General appeared. I dared not stutter.

"You speak better today," remarked the professor.

"Sir, I was nervous."

The General smiled behind his fan-shaped beard, but I was again under arrest to cure my nerves.

Happily arrests were exceptional. Usually I left college at 5 P.M., ran through my home work and prepared to enjoy life.

St. Petersburg was at that time a world centre of musical and dramatic ability. Apart from our great Russian artists, singers and actors came from all over the world to this capital which gave them a reception and an understanding they could find nowhere else. But owing to the high standard of its own productions, Petrograd tolerated only the best. Sham, forced talent with no soul behind it did not bluff the Russian public. At the Moscow Arts Theatre no actor walked on until he had studied for three years. Plays were rehearsed for two years before Stanislavski considered them ready for the public. The technique of our ballet had taken generations to perfect and we judged artists according to the standards of Chaliapin, Sobinof, Davidoff and Dalmatoff. Caruso came to Petrograd, but Russian critics did not think he could compete with Masini. Isadora Duncan had a mild success. We were always ready for new things, but her emotional unrestraint rather palled beside the trained intellectuality of our ballet.

Italian opera became very popular and a company from the Comédie Française played throughout the season. Among the foreign stars I saw in my page days were Coquelin (in *Cyrano de Bergerac*), Rejane, Battistini, Dux, Cotoni, Zembrich, Auer, Patti (in her last days) and the two strange women who towered in their different ways above the rest, Eleanora Duse and Sarah Bernhardt.

From the age of fourteen we of the Corps and other schools were encouraged to go to concerts and theatres twice a week. Instead of Hollywood film stars the artists mentioned above moulded our taste. I was no exception. The much-criticized "retrograde and obscure Russian Government" arranged for all students of gymnasiums, universities and military academies to have half-price tickets or free entry to operas and theatres. Boys and girls, rich and poor, met in the common-room of art and were taught to care for beauty at the most impressionable age. Sitting with friends in the upper circle I learnt to appreciate and criticize the theatre. It was my first contact with a world where talent meant more than happiness.

Apart from concerts and operas we saw plays performed to absolute perfection, and perfection in any craft stirs and inspires the onlookers. Genius was required even in the smallest part, and as a result I was spoilt for theatres outside my own country. Perhaps Russians have a natural aptitude for acting as they have for music; anyhow they have infinite capacity for work, know how to blend technique with talent, how to discover and reveal the Russian soul.

In these days of stupendous films and settings costing thousands I cannot but be *blasé*, for never does one equal the glamorous reality of a first night in Petrograd or Moscow.

The Imperial Ballet reached its apogee during these years. Pavlova and Karsavina were still in the corps de ballet but when the

chance of a pas seul occurred they thrilled more than the older
and technically more perfect ballerinas. I made friends with
Nicolas Legat, the trainer of Pavlova and Nijinsky, and himself
one of the greatest dancers of all time, and when there was time
he let me come to rehearsals.

I saw the fiasco of Tchekoff's *Seagull* presented for the first time
at the Alexandrine Theatre. The younger generation liked this
play better than their elders. I can't believe we understood it, but
then I knew and loved Davidoff and Varlarmoff, the great actors
who were personal friends and often came to Mother's house.

Curiously, the younger generation, the schoolboys, liked this
strange new type of play, which showed to perfection the suffering, paralysed soul of Russian intellectual gentry—a soul that
died with the nineteenth century, for with the early 1900's national reforms swept Russia forward to what, it seemed, was
going to be a wave of vigorous, joyous art.

Most of the pages by now had a secret romance. After sudden infatuations at Christmas parties now came a new kind of
abstract love. We grew moody and jealous over ballerinas we'd
never met. With wistful enthusiasm photos of ethereal dancers
were hidden in prayer-books. And the more we yearned, the more
we tried to hide our feeling by loudly expressing our scorn for all
women.

So five years rolled by.

Paul Rodzianko (in lace dress) with brothers and sister.

Rodzianko (right) and his family.

The Emperor and the Empress in Moscow.

Rodzianko's parents dressed for the court ball. Petrograd, 1903.

Rodzianko's father as the commander of a Cossack regiment in the Caucasus.

Rodzianko in his first car.
With Prince Alexander Chavchavadze, Petrograd, 1903.

A regimental lunch given to the Chevalier Guards by the horse guards.
Krasnoe Selo, 1906.

The Grand Duchesses Olga and Tatiana in the uniform of their regiments (3rd Elisavetgradski Hussars and 8th Vosnesenki Lancers).

The Empress with two of her children.

*The Emperor with the
Tzarevitch.*

*The Empress Marie
in the uniform of
her regiment of the
Chevalier Guard.*

Rodzianko in the uniform of the Chevalier Guard.

The Tzar and Tzarina receiving veterans of 1812 during the celebrations of the Battle of Borodino.

Rodzianko on "Jenga," King Edward VII. Cup at Olympia, 1912.

Rodzianko on Macgillycuddy o' the Reeks. King Edward VII. Cup, 1913, 1914.

CHAPTER 5

Military Training, Marriage &
Some Account of Pre-War Paris

At eighteen I was promoted to the senior section of the Corps des Pages, which corresponded to Sandhurst training. We were now considered as being on active service and special military studies replaced ordinary education. We took more interest in our chest expansion however than in technical examinations. Young, healthy, full of ambition, the pages stood at attention for hours, drilled, dreamed of future glories and developed into proud, loyal, muscular men. Brave, yes, and cultured; hardened by military training, taught to laugh at death—yet in a way their lives had been as sheltered, as set to routine as those of their sisters. They were trained to fight and die according to a traditional, noble pattern. For the bitter mercenary struggle for bread and butter that lay ahead they could not have been more pathetically equipped. Indeed, when the time came, the women of Russia adapted themselves skilfully, for they could sew, teach, open hat shops. But the remnant of officers who escaped could not join the armies of other nations, and that was all they were fit for. The Russian in his heart is indifferent to material wealth, and Western Civilization scorns his inability to cope with the practical side of life.

I was among those selected for the Hon. Degree of Pages to His Majesty's Court. On special occasions we were called to court

to carry the trains of the Empress and Grand Duchesses. These
occasions were rare, for the Empress was shy and disliked public functions. A devoted wife and mother she wished only for a
quiet existence with her children. These domestic tastes lowered
her prestige. She was Empress of All the Russias and the crowd
wanted spectacle! When she did appear, tall, straight and beautiful, the people shouted their lungs out, but they saw her seldom,
and these reticent ways made her unpopular.

Even the pages longed for more occasions to show off their fine
uniforms in front of Her Majesty's lovely maids of honour.

Every Sunday at church I wore the dress uniform and clanking
spurs and sword which were my greatest pride. I couldn't resist
clattering as I handed around the collection plate, and prayers
were disturbed. The priest requested Kamer-Page Rodzianko to
wear smaller spurs during service.

Mother gave me a tandem of white horses which I drove
around the capital, and altogether life was going very pleasantly
when at a court ball I met the most beautiful girl of the season, Tamara Novosilzoff, a maid of honour to the two Empresses
and daughter of the Commander of a Cossack regiment of the
Guards. I proposed and, to my delighted surprise, was accepted.

Not having finished the military college I had no right to get
engaged, but General Novosilzoff, having served in the same regiment as the Tzar, obtained His Majesty's special permission.

At the beginning of August the Emperor personally promoted
me to be Second Lieutenant in the Chevalier Guards, and at the
end of the same month I was married.

All Petrograd seemed to be in the church; the Grand Dukes
Vladimir and Cyril, and the Grand Duchess Marie, and Grand
Duke Constantine promised, somewhat prematurely, to be god-
father to my first son (which he eventually was). And Queen Olga
of Greece was also present, and most of the diplomatic corps,
hundreds of fellow officers and many Ukrainian countrymen.

My great-uncle, fat Prince Kotchubey, descendant of the famous Kotchubey in the opera *Mazeppa*, drank an enormous cup

of nectar and smashed the glass down for good luck. Russians when happy always break things.

That evening we left for the Ukraine and spent our honeymoon at the Wolf's Den. I continued the usual sporting life, riding through the forests, swimming and shooting. Actually I never enjoyed shooting any animals except wolves, and have yet to see what can be called "sport" in killing a creature that is not fierce enough to fight back. One day in the forest I got very near to a deer. I was sure she saw me yet she did not run away, she stared straight at me with soft brown eyes. A shame came over me that I, whom nothing attacked, should seek to destroy this soft creature when I was not even hungry. In fox-hunting one at least risks breaking one's neck. A "game" is the surmounting of artificial barriers for the fun of the thing, such as jumping, a complicated idea only common to civilized humans, but no game becomes "sport" without an element of danger.

Years later, during the war, when German bombs were dropping and men falling in heaps, I thought of pheasant shoots and wondered if this could be our "Karma," and that what one makes others feel one has to feel oneself, or was it like "sport," just another manifestation of human nature?

But to return to the Wolf's Den. There was not much for a girl to do in the country and my wife spent most of her time playing the piano. She belonged to the age when girls took their music out to dinner and, when begged to perform, would plead sore throats and then give endless dull encores. It was not so bad in Russia because they almost all had lovely voices, but Tamara's soprano held the most critical spellbound.

In Russia, girls were brought up most strictly and almost over-educated. Unlike their contemporaries in English school-rooms, where dear old governesses drowsed and dreamed, here they had expert tuition morning, noon and night and had to speak three or four languages perfectly. For some unearthly reason all were anxious to pass the difficult examinations giving the right to be a teacher. This necessitated hard study and nerve strain during the years of adolescence and by the age of seventeen, when they came out, many girls were over developed mentally, inclined to be unbalanced and nervous. My own sister was seriously ill from work after getting her diploma.

Then straight from the grind of the school-room a girl was brought out, presented and plunged into court life. Their scintillating intellectuality made Russian women doubly attractive later on, but the girls were quite unprepared for the gay life opened to them. At court balls they were suddenly surrounded by handsome and interested young officers on the look-out for new charm and beauty. After a number of proposals they would marry the one they thought best-looking, or one sought after by other girls and a few years later would be surprised to find themselves really quite unsuited.

In Russia marriages only took place in church; civil registration was not necessary, so that if a divorce was wanted only the priest arranged it. Divorce was much more frequent than at that period in England and no stigma was attached to divorced parties. Also, in a thing so personal as marriage, justice could often be dispensed better by a priest who had probably known both parties since childhood, than in a court of law.

At the Wolf's Den the romantic life soon began to pall. We left for Paris, still the most glamorous city of Europe. The streets were full of laughter and excitement as if during a perpetual festival. Millionaires of all countries, gay old dogs and young officers, royal princes and the world's most lovely cocottes all flocked to Paris. Every man who had a penny to spend and wanted a good time came to this mad cosmopolitan city.

The boulevards sang with the pleasure of living. At every café sat exotically clad ladies as remarkable for their beauty as for their lack of virtue. To their escorts they talked in every language, with all accents, blondes, brunettes and red-heads. Blue eyes and green smiled alluringly and diamonds glittered on the slim brown fingers of southern climes. Hats at that time were huge and befeathered. Parisiennes wore voluptuous gowns, incredible ruffles and seemed hung with furs, flowers and ostrich plumes. Their light banter, strange eyes and naughty painted lips rather impressed me, but though friends often called me to a table and introduced me, their appraising eyes made one too shy to speak. Feeling larger than ever, I sat with one foot on top of another and tried to keep my hands from knocking glasses over.

The cafés of Paris remain, but gone is that race of mysterious, wicked goddesses of fun. Today a successful cocotte immediately wants to turn into a lady and join polite society. The old type laid a barrier between themselves and the world, which made them much more exciting.

I remember walking along in a pensive mood when a taxi nearly ran me down. "Vous ne sortez que les dimanche?" yelled the driver and was out of sight.

With fellow officers I went to the Bal Tabarin, and on one occasion that now seems fantastic and unbelievable we visited the Moulin Rouge. The famous music-hall was packed with prosperous, slightly intoxicated gentlemen in evening dress, all showing off and thinking themselves tremendous devils. There were tables around the dance floor and champagne flowed literally in all directions. The usual assortment of glamorous women gazed tenderly into the glazing eyes of their swains and fifty *cancan* girls kicked on the stage.

Strolling into Maxim's, the famous restaurant which was my father's favourite haunt, I was given a great reception on his account. "Le fils du General Rodzianko . . . Oh mais oui, Monsieur . . ." The Rodzianko March "Cassez Tout" was struck up and I learnt that my father's parties were as famous in Paris as in Petrograd.

Members of the family were not asked except fat Prince Kotchubey, who was so busy eating he never looked at pretty ladies. Kotchubey had been very rich but he literally ate away his fortune, and came to an untimely end. He was an extraordinary character, intelligent and well-read. He collected a fine library, but apart from literature only food seemed to interest him. I often visited him in the country, for his conversation was brilliant, but meals lasted a couple of hours and, being in training, I could not waste time at table. He ate more than anyone I ever saw, but it did not seem to affect his brain.

Poor uncle paid for his greed. One hot day when travelling in the Ukraine he stopped at a tavern, drank too much cold beer and burst on the way home! We always thought it a very funny end.

CHAPTER 6

The Chevalier Guards &
the Emperor Nicolas II

In November my leave came to an end and returning to Petrograd I began service in earnest. It was good to have real work to do after hanging around restaurants and dressmakers. The social life in Petrograd reached its peak that year, for after the Japanese War entertaining was naturally reduced. We did not take a house of our own but lived in a section of my parents' large house. The court balls were splendid and Mother gave several big parties, but I did not care for society and devoted all my thoughts and energy to the Army. The Emperor gave the famous ball when the court were clad in the dress of the time of Ivan the Terrible, and Mother had all her diamonds made into a gorgeous breastplate. My wife wore the family sapphires, my sister, Princess Chavchavadze, the emeralds and my brother Alex's wife (*née* Countess Narishkine) the rubies. The ball was a barbaric and wonderful sight.

Every morning I got up at six and went to the barracks, where I trained and worked till evening. My life became as regular as it had been in the Corps des Pages.

It was real and thrilling work. I liked and understood the young soldiers in my charge, for they were mostly Ukrainians. The best, most reliable soldiers came from that part of Russia. Apart from drilling the recruits, I often had to teach them the alphabet, for the men were great big children, chosen for their physique. Magnificent specimens and fearless hunters in their own wild forests, they were dazed by Petrograd and incredibly simple.

One day I found a huge Siberian weeping in a barracks yard.

"What on earth's the matter?"

"Sir, I can't find my squadron barracks."

Hercules looked woefully down at me.

"But you are standing in front of the door. Can't you read the notice?"

"No, sir; I'm not used to finding my way by funny signs."

Thanking me profusely, he went to his quarters. In the wild he would have been at home.

This was the type of man that Russia used in time of war. They died in thousands, idealistically, senselessly, and when revolution came they were puzzled, depressed, swept in the tide—without even understanding.

I repeat that the northern Russians were less reliable fighters than the Ukrainians. This sturdy race with healthy climate, plentiful food and Cossack upbringing, produces about the finest specimens and staunchest fighters in the world. I am over six-foot, but when drilling my squadron I felt like a pigmy. The men were well-proportioned and physically fearless, but Balzac wrote truly, "Il y a souvent de l'enfant chez le soldat et presque toujours du soldat chez l'enfant."

Apart from technical training we had a lot of drill and gymnastics. I taught some of my squadron to walk on their hands and sing at the same time. They liked to show off this unorthodox exercise on every possible occasion.

The officers fenced daily and I began to work seriously at sports. In the winter months the squadron rode and skied on the frozen Neva, the crisp snow crackling under our weight.

When the men worked well Sunday treats were organized. The soldiers were sent to see museums, factories, theatres and circuses, which, being ignorant of any way of life save their own villages, they enjoyed immensely.

The greatest attraction of all proved to be the French wrestling at the circuses, which they afterwards practised among themselves. As all my time and thoughts were entirely devoted to the men, they worked well and came out top in competitions and examinations.

Food in the Army was rich and plentiful. New men unaccustomed to it overate as a result. There was one particularly unfortunate Shrove Tuesday when, like greedy schoolboys, the soldiers tried to see who could eat most pancakes. On top of it all they drank beer and vodka which fermented, and some even died.

These sorts of disasters seem to happen to no other nation. Who said that Russians could tighten their belts and starve longer than any other race, just as, when the time came, they could eat and drink more?

On Christmas Eve, service was held in the Regimental church. I can remember the strange exuberance of that evening; the far off cold stars in the sky, a light snow falling and the bells ringing through the frosty night.

The church was white inside and the warm air laden with incense. The altar doors glittered and the priests moved slowly in their heavy robes. Dark-faced ikons gazed inscrutably into the Russian souls before them. One by one the soldiers came in, their faces glowing from the cold outside and their white tunics flecked with snow. The deep voices of the choir burst forth in peace and magnificence.

The soldiers were very religious. Their husky faces changed when praying and earnestness shone in their eyes. Each man placed a lighted candle before his chosen ikon, and said a silent prayer before going out. Never in my travels since have I seen men so strong and beautiful and simple of soul.

After the service a huge tree was lit up in the regimental riding school. On it hung gifts for every man from the officers. Then came displays by acrobats and conjurers, until dawn whitened the sky and a wintry sun gilded the domes of the snow-covered city.

It was all very charming and romantic. Officers and men seemed to understand each other and share the same interests.

But how it was to crash, that simple life, when outside influences bore down, when all these tall fair men were dead and conscription swept a new type into their barracks.

Maybe it still stands, that white church in Petrograd, but on Christmas Eve it is dark and empty. Ukrainian soldiers still fill the ranks of the new Red Army, for the best fighters will always come from the South, but when the time arrives and Russia goes to war again will they fight as they did for their Little Father?

I wonder.

Once a month we had a regimental dinner. There was a certain amount of drinking, but no more than in other countries. The debauched life of pre-war has been ridiculously exaggerated by films and musical comedies, and the most fanciful legends have resulted. Educated Englishmen ask me, "But before the war you had *droit du seigneur* in Russia?"

"No," I answer—"Why, did you?"

This does not seem to please them.

After the regimental dinner the doors were flung open and military bands or Tziganes came in and played. Then the regimental singers marched in and stood to attention before the commanding officer.

"How are you, little brothers?"

"We wish you health, Excellency!" they answered in a shout.

Then, standing legs apart, they took a deep breath and a cloud of sound filled the room, their strong, natural voices growing fierce and sad by turns.

When it was my squadron's turn they marched in on their hands, singing lustily all the time. This feat invariably got enormous applause and made the men train more eagerly than ever. Some of them had wonderful voices, of a timbre I never hear now except perhaps in the Russian Church in Paris, or in some restaurant where a soldier earns his daily bread with nightly song. I generally returned from the regimental dinners, which have been so luridly depicted in Hollywood films, intoxicated with music rather than wine.

It was not the debauchery of the upper classes that led to the downfall of the Russian Empire, nor were the workers abused or the peasants bullied, nor was the Government retrograde; it made enormous strides in the new century. It was simply that Russia was too huge, too childish, too poorly organized to be able to go to war outside her borders. The very vastness that saved her from invasion and defeated Napoleon, proved her own destruction. Enormous fronts, loosely hung together, sapped her best men and prepared the way for a revolution.

About twice a month I was sent on guard duty at the Winter Palace. The soldiers with me were wide-shouldered Ukrainians whom I had to look up to when giving orders. We were dressed in white tunics with silver facings, blue trousers, high boots and spurs, a sword clanking at the side and double-headed eagle on our helmets.

Guard duty lasted twenty-four hours at a stretch. Headquarters were in the Field-Marshal's Hall near the Emperor's study. At night we stood outside his bedroom. Sentries were posted two at a time at the doors. I sent the men off to sleep in parties but was not supposed to rest myself. After twelve hours uniforms got very uncomfortable. A number of Ethiopian servants lived in the Palace, and one of them brought us coffee every few hours. With relief we heard the clanging footsteps of the change of guard on the following noon.

The Tzar often came out of his study and stopped to talk in his friendly way. His wide education had given him a charmingly easy manner, especially among soldiers, for he had studied the art of war and served in each of the three arms. As a young man he had not felt himself suitable to be Emperor and begged his father to let him abdicate in favour of his brother the Grand Duke Michael. But Alexander III refused to listen. When the time came Nicolas tried to stifle his doubt in himself, took up the burden and faced the future bravely. His tastes remained extremely simple and he was the kindest of men. When I was on guard the first time, he happened to appear unexpectedly when the soldiers were sitting at ease in the Great Hall. We leapt to our feet and my helmet, which I had removed, crashed to the ground.

The Tzar saw my embarrassment, and as I nervously picked the damn thing up and put it on, he laughed.

"Don't worry, Rodzianko. These things happen."

This small incident mattered so much at the time. The smile in his hazel eyes saved me and my men much anguish.

His Majesty knew many soldiers by name and was always asking them details of their family life and how things were going on in their homes. In this way he learnt something of village life in his Empire. It is rather hard to describe the tone in which Russian officers talked to their men, because I have never come across that exact relationship in the armies of other countries. Except when actually giving orders we did not assume a military note; we talked almost as if to children, confidentially, simply, using often Christian names. An English soldier might resent his General asking questions about his family life, chaffing him on the number of children, hoping his sweetheart is pretty. The Englishman's home is his castle and his own business, but the Russian soldier likes to tell his General that the wife is expecting another. The best officers knew details about their men that in other countries might be considered foolish. For instance, most of the men came from far away and sometimes they got worried about their wives' faithfulness. In this state a man does not make a good soldier; it is no good punishing him, his mind is not on the job. It is the officer's business to find out what worries him and help him set it to rights, though I am afraid that officers giving advice on the delicate subject of women were sometimes rather worried by their own wives! The attitude of officers to men is perfectly shown in the usual form of address, "Bratzi," ("Little brothers") or "Molodzi" ("Brave youths"). My men adored their Little Father, but most of them died far from him.

I wish I could remember more of the Emperor's conversations, he was always so kind and human; but few actual words stick in my memory. The thing he said oftenest to me was, "Never mind. It doesn't matter," because I always seemed to be doing things wrong! Misfortunes dogged my path. One evening my regiment were invited to dinner at the Palace with the Emperor. It was the sort of grand event when young officers take care to behave themselves. I choked explosively on the first mouthful, and vainly tried to sip a glass of water while my partner patted my back. It went on, louder and louder. A few Generals tried to continue conversation, but it became impossible against my gasping coughs. The whole table was reduced to embarrassed silence. Tears rolled down my purple countenance and yet the convulsions continued. Everyone looked annoyed except His Majesty, who had to remember that kings cannot laugh when their subjects choke! When at last I reached the stage of silent blushes he smiled and said "Hard luck" before resuming the conversation with a glowering Field-Marshal.

During levees we wore red cuirasses decorated with two large stars, and tight white leather trousers. One night during a great ball I had to be on guard in this stiff uniform from 8 P.M. till 3 A.M. I was rather vain about my figure, but one tailor tried too hard and made a new cuirass so tight that I could hardly breathe. Glasses of brandy kept me on my feet. The ladies walking about in ball dresses looked at my set face through lorgnettes, and as through a mist I heard voices say, "Poor fellow, how pale he looks!"

No wonder girls with small waists were always fainting!

The biggest event of the year, the Parade of Guards, took place in May on the Champs de Mars. What a grand sight! The Cossack Guards in scarlet, the Ataman Cossacks in brilliant blue, the Chevalier Guards and Horse Guards glittering in the sun as if clad in golden armour. The Tzar rode to the grandstand, the Empress following in a *calèche* drawn by eight albino horses with pink eyes. It was a scene from a fairy story. The day ended with a huge cavalry charge that stopped short in front of the royal box. As a little boy I was taken to see the parade and for years I took part in it, but I never grew less impressed, the thrill of the charge never palled. It was not merely military pageant, gorgeous theatre, it was the flower of Russia riding as they would ride to their deaths.

Apart from military events and court receptions, all went on quietly at home. My wife was delicate and the house smelt of chloroform and medicine. Occasionally she came down to the piano and sang duets with Battistini, the famous baritone, who admired her voice greatly.

Many operas and theatrical receptions were given at the Hermitage Theatre to which the Emperor invited the court, the Diplomatic Corps and Guards officers, as well as many others. These plays were always followed by supper in the Winter Palace. Outside, the Palace Square would be filled with waiting carriages, horses and coachmen, and owing to the terrific cold a huge fire was lit around which they crowded and drank hot tea.

When summer came I startled my family by buying a motorcar, one of the first in Petrograd. It was a Richard-Brassier, and before an admiring crowd I would drive fellow officers down to the camp. Bumping along country roads, horses who had never seen such a thing would go mad and crowds frequently collected.

Our house was open to all the artists, and in this way I grew friendly with the greatest actors and singers of the world. Feodor Chaliapin often came to my parties and sang. The Imperial Theatre was unique. Apart from ballet one saw there performances of incredible perfection. No other countries have ever had such acting, such singing, such tense expectancy on the part of the audience.

Petrograd was always ready to judge and welcome anything new. After Tchekoff Gorky appeared, and Gorky was as new to us as Zola was to Paris. I remember going to see *The Lower Depths* with an officer of my regiment, Paul Skoropadsky, who was later to become Hetman of the Ukraine. Gorky's play was pretty drawing-room stuff compared to what we would one day see of human nature.

One Sunday I was sitting alone at home when Andrew B——, my friend, an officer of the Lancers, was announced. He entered in a great state, stuttering more than usual: "P-P-Paul, my wife has left me and I've got five days' leave from Warsaw to get her back."

I tried to calm him and get the story straight. It appeared that his young wife was entirely dominated by her mother, who had

settled herself to live with them in Warsaw and made perpetual
trouble. Finally, after a row the mother insisted on her daughter
leaving my friend and coming to Petrograd with her small baby.

Poor Andrew was desperate. "My wife is all right," he explained,
"only my mother-in-law can't stand me, and is always saying I'm
not good enough for her daughter."

"Well, what on earth can I do?"

"Be a good chap," he pleaded. "Go and see my wife and ask her
to come back to me. She likes you."

I agreed, and an hour later called at the apartment of Andrew's
mother-in-law. Her daughter was in and saw me at once, a sweet,
pretty woman with large eyes and gentle mouth, obviously under
Mother's influence.

I reasoned with her and she admitted she loved her husband.
All her arguments began, "But Mother says . . . But Mother won't
allow . . ."

Seeing how the land lay, I admired the mewling baby and departed.

Next day my solicitor told me that the father had equal legal
right to the child with the mother, and here I thought to break
down the enemy's defence.

I gave my friend orders to sit in a cab outside his mother-in-
law's house until he saw that lady take her daughter out for their
daily walk.

"B-B-B-But I've only f-five days . . ."

"Obey my orders and so to victory," I commanded.

Then I got my friend Prince Amiloghvari to lend us his flat in
the barracks of the Cossacks of the Guards, and from the reg-
istered agency I got a foster nurse for the child. The nurse was
installed in the flat and told to await events. The sentries were
ordered to let no one pass except me and B——.

According to orders, the bereaved husband discovered when
his wife went out walking with her mother, and as soon as they
were out of sight rang the door bell. When the door opened he
pushed past the maid and tore up to the room where he knew the

baby lay. Brushing aside the bewildered nurse, he wrapt the child up and ran downstairs and off to Amiloghvari's flat.

Knowing all this, I waited expectantly at home. Sure enough the telephone rang and Mme B——'s tearful voice quavered: "Oh, Lieutenant Rodzianko, my baby's been stolen" (sniff, sniff). "My husband stole it . . . What shall I do? Help me. My mother is furious . . . absolutely furious. She says she is setting the police after you."

I told her not to worry, that the father had equal legal right to the child, that her mother did not interest me, but I would like to see her alone.

Half an hour later she appeared with eyes that would melt a heart of stone and began sobbing about her baby's starvation and death. I told her the child was with a good foster mother.

"Oh, my mother is furious . . ." she began again.

"Who did you marry anyway?" I asked. "You've got a nice good-looking fellow even if he does stutter a bit, and you can't treat a man like that. Make up your mind definitely. If you wish to see the child it can be arranged, but you must decide now between your mother and your husband."

Unexpectedly she changed. "You're right. I'll go back to him."

I rang up Andrew, who literally whooped with joy and took his wife around to the barracks past the stiffly saluting though amazed sentry.

In a short time the quarrel was patched up and the couple decided the child was to be christened next day and I would be god-father. "And your mother god-mother?" I suggested.

"N-N-N-No, b-b-but . . ." spluttered Andrew.

Anyway I was in the thick of the affair. They sent me around to explain to the mother-in-law . . . a jolly task! She received me coldly, refused to shake hands, but agreed to come to the christening.

I warned B—— never to let the baby out of his sight. The christening passed with mixed feelings, and on the fifth day I saw them off on the train for Warsaw. B—— had his wife, the wife had her baby, and all looked radiant except mother-in-law, who cast me looks indescribable.

Soon after Andrew resigned from his regiment and the couple settled in the Caucasus, where I visited them. Andrew died of consumption seven years later, and among his last words was a laughing "Thank Paul . . ."

CHAPTER 7

Japanese War & Revolution of 1904

For twenty years Russia had known peace. Internal troubles having died down, the country was gaining strength and developing rapidly when, in 1904, the Japanese War broke out. I was on guard at the Winter Palace when the news came through. We did not take it seriously. Most people laughed at the idea of little cheeky Japan daring to stand up to invincible Russia. We all had the old-fashioned idea of war as a glorious chance for brave exploits and personal heroism and the officers of the Chevalier Guards clamoured to go to the front immediately. We drew lots; I was among those who had to stay. Already there was a fear that Germany might move if too many troops left the capital. As the war progressed the Kaiser, being nervous of Japan, promised not to invade Russia.

For a time Petrograd hardly noticed that war was on, but many of the officers who went off to Manchuria as if to a picnic never returned, and soon the perpetual retreats of our Army made us realize something must be very wrong.

Our tactics were old-fashioned, our guns of antiquated design; the Russian Army fought in coloured uniforms, whereas the Japanese wore khaki. Enormous casualties naturally resulted, and the brilliant morale of the men was worn down by perpetual retreats and unnecessary losses owing to incompetence of commanding officers. A single line of communication across Siberia increased difficulties. As the General Staff realized that great changes must be speedily effected, many commanders were replaced, but during this reorganization the Army continued to retire. The country knew too well the seriousness of the situation. Gradually things improved, but ill-luck seemed to dog us. The Tzar made long journeys to bless the departing troops and give them ikons, but the range of Japanese guns was better than ours, and that mattered more to the ranks.

In August 1904 the long-awaited Tzarevitch was born and Nicolas asked all who had been on the battlefield to be honorary godfathers, but this did not appease men who felt that they were being used as cannon fodder. Meanwhile our fleet went around Africa to try to save Port Arthur. At Tsu-Shima they met the Japanese and were almost wiped out. Many Russian battleships were sunk and thousands of lives lost. My brother Vladimir was second-in-command on board the special service ship *Irtish*. His ship was hit but floated for a time before sinking. The crew escaped in the boats which were not smashed or burnt by gunfire. Being picked up by the Japanese, my brother spent a very interesting time in captivity. The Japanese treated officers extremely well and Vladimir had all kinds of entertainment, including, I believe, a charming little Japanese wife.

The defeat at Tsu-Shima caused resentment among all classes in Western Russia. The ground being ploughed for trouble, revolutionary propaganda sprang up, discontent not being confined to the lower classes. This was the moment that subversive powers had waited for. From factories and universities, wherever propaganda could be easily distributed, revolutionary doctrines spread all over Russia. Disturbances in Petrograd were led by the unsavoury priest Gapon (an ex-secret-agent who had become a Revolutionary Socialist and ended by being hanged by the revolutionaries themselves as a traitor). Regiments spent most of the time on duty. The atmosphere grew tense and unpleasant. In Petrograd the Guards were kept busy owing to riots. Occasionally there were scraps, but the crowds even when egged on by agita-

tors were good-natured. Often the police got nervous and antag-
onized the people, when a little tact would have worked wonders.
Of course the masses changed when the Big Revolt came, with
hunger and terror. I am afraid the revolutionary leaders learned
more psychology than we did during this try-out.

One winter morning, several hours before dawn, I was sent out
with my squadron to clear away a crowd which had collected in
a large Square.

As we jogged through the silent streets a police officer came up
nervously and asked me to charge the crowd:

"Why?"

"They refuse to disperse."

"Can't you argue with them?"

"It's no use. They are getting insulting."

Convinced he had behaved tactlessly, I refused to charge without provocation. Threatening to report me to the Commander,
the police officer went off seething.

Having led my squadron to the Square, I left them 100 yards
behind and approached the silent crowd, who obviously awaited
action.

"Good morning, fellows," I yelled, "aren't you cold standing
here this icy morning? If you're not, I am. Look at this man with
icicles on his beard like Father Christmas."

This childish joke aroused a few laughs and they began to
listen.

"It is my duty to disperse you, but surely no-one will give any
trouble."

"We can talk to this fellow," shouted one of the leaders. A
clamour of ill-defined complaints arose, but I simply asked them
to help us soldiers by going off to their homes. With a few jokes
this ruse succeeded. After a tricky moment they agreed to depart.

"I give you twenty minutes and trust you; but of course, when
that time has elapsed I shall be forced to take measures. Please
help me do my duty."

I retired as if taking it for granted they would go. Twenty minutes later not a soul remained in the Square. The people were

like the soldiers, to be reasoned with as children, but dangerous and stupid when roused. Beneath glamour, magnificence and tradition the structure of that great Empire was smouldering even then. It could have been rebuilt internally if only the war had not come; but "ifs" are fruitless.

The famous Sunday, January 9, 1905, proved different. I was on guard with my regiment on the left side of the Winter Palace when the crowd of thousands of workmen, excited by revolutionary leaders, filled the Square, shouting and swearing. The agitators knew the Tzar was away at Tzarskoie Selo and the march could only have been organized to make trouble. After several hours the police failed to disperse the mob; the clamour did not abate, nor would the people listen when told the Tzar was not in the Palace. Insults were hurled, and finally towards dusk our Commanding Officer ordered the trumpeter to give the signal to charge. Owing to 15° of frost the trumpet was frozen and only gave a splutter. It was extremely funny and we laughed with the crowd. As the first line charged, the crowd lay down and the horses stopped dead and skidded, to the discomfort of the riders, many of whom almost came off; being immediately behind, we saw a line of cavalrymen shoot onto their horses' necks and could hardly sit in our saddles with laughter.

Wheeling the horses with difficulty owing to the slippery ground, the officers managed to back their horses onto the crowd, which surged back and soon dispersed in spite of agitators shouting, as usual, in the rear, well out of harm's way.

Meanwhile, the other side of the Palace, the Preobrajensky Regiment had been forced to fire and 70 men were killed.

We heard the shots but did not know till later what had occurred. From the second line of the Chevalier Guards I had a good view of the comic side of the situation, but I must say the sensation of charging an unarmed crowd was unpleasant.

A month later the Grand Duke Serge was assassinated and his wife (the Empress's sister) became a nun. In June the Black Sea Fleet mutinied, and after the fall of Port Arthur, de Witte advised the Emperor to make peace with Japan. Witte departed for U.S.A. and signed the Treaty of Portsmouth just as the Russian Army felt itself ready technically and morally for another blow at the enemy. Disappointed and disgruntled at an Armistice just when they did not want it, the Russian troops slowly returned to the West. Mutinies and general strikes sprang up but were suppressed.

Longing to fight, the men came back to find the revolution sizzling. The Tzar issued his famous manifesto establishing an Imperial Parliament; in other words, it was the first step to granting a Constitution to the people of Russia. Many members of Trotsky's First Soviet were arrested and 1906 came in grimly with terrorist organizations retaliating against the Government by a series of political assassinations.

But numerous plots were frustrated and as quietness returned we continued our way of life unthinking.

Queen Olga of Greece (granddaughter of Nicolas I) spent much of her time in Russia, and often lunching with her, I came to know her charming grandson, the present King of Greece. I remember a delightful story Queen Olga told against herself. In those days when a train of ammunition carts passed through the streets the first cart always carried a red flag as warning to passers-by not to smoke or throw lighted matches. Queen Olga seeing one of these carts, thought it a revolutionary demonstration and asked a policeman why he allowed it. How she laughed when told it was merely a danger signal.

Happiness is the most illogical thing in this world. At that time I possessed every material asset, yet I was restless and heavy at heart.

Social life bored me. The luxury of my home I did not heed, and glimpses of the art and talent of Petrograd merely increased my longing to achieve something.

My parents had their country places to organize, and even with the help of a good agent this took much of their time. They built hospitals in every village and small railways across the estates. All over Russia fresh country was being opened up and under the new reforms the peasants thrived. Old Strogonoff had left estates the size of Yorkshire with hundreds of square miles of forest that had not been touched since Ivan the Terrible had given it to our ancestor four centuries before.

While cutting away the forest at Usviat in the province of Vitebsk (where Ney's army had retired in the retreat from Moscow), some of our men discovered a clearing in which lay nearly 1000 human skeletons. We realized they must be a troop of French soldiers who had lost their way and perished from cold and starvation. By the bayonets and military buttons we sent to Paris they identified the regiment which had lain there for nearly a hundred years.

We still spent summers at the "Wolf's Den," and during my leaves I would travel to one of our country places. My tame bears were adorable, fearless and quite safe. I never enjoyed bear shooting or killing, but occasionally it was necessary and several babies were brought back to me. Sentiment apart, the peasant's way of killing bears was a thrilling sport. In winter the bears go to sleep under snow, generally in a hole in the roots of a fallen tree in the forest. The steam of their warm breath coming through a little hole shows where they lie. The forester watches and marks the place a bear chooses for the winter sleep. Then one hunter with a *rogatin*, a special hunting spear, rouses him up. Sleepy and furious the animal wakes, rears on his hind legs (bears stand 6 to 8 feet) and charges. The man spears him and the bear in anger would seize the iron bar and draw the knife into himself. Men were often killed in this sport and it took a game fellow to tackle the bear. With guns there was less danger, unless the bear was wounded.

Bears are naturally clean and in summer mine ran about the house and played with my two younger brothers. Mishka, my own special pet, travelled with me in trains and slept in my study. They romped with the dogs, but I could never get horses accustomed to them, so the stables were *verboten*. Mishka, a most intelligent rascal, had a liking for beer, which he drank solemnly out of the bottle, sitting on his hind legs. One day he ventured half a mile away where a man kept a little grocery-shop in a hut. In he strolled and put his paws on the counter, sniffing expectantly. The terrified owner had an open bottle on hand, which he gave him. Mishka drained it and walked out. Next day he returned and the next and the next. Knowing what he wanted, the shop-keeper dared not refuse it. I received a pathetic note asking if the bear could be stopped. The poor animal's grunting efforts to talk were taken for threatening growls. Mishka enjoyed his shop-ping expeditions, however, so I ordered the beer to be put on my account and in time he was regarded as a good customer.

The only disaster occurred when a bear went to the kitchen for a tit-bit and a new maid got frightened and threw a jug of boiling water on him. Naturally this made the animal cross, but other-wise they were perfectly trustworthy and even my small children played with them.

Bears aren't affectionate in the same sense as dogs; they did not mope when I went away, but they always remembered one and seemed quite as intelligent. They knew perfectly well it was naughty to steal and used to run away very fast if I appeared, climb to the top of a tree and sit there laughing. The only way to train a bear is by a smart smack on the nose the very instant he has done wrong; five minutes after is too late and only irri-tates him.

The servants got used to them and reported misdeeds just as if they were, children. It was almost "Master Mishka has stolen a pot of jam, sir." I would go out and try to catch the ruffian, who was generally sitting at the foot of a tall tree eating for all he was worth and watching out of the corner of his eye to see me com-ing. Instantly he would drop the pot and was away up the tree till evening.

One day the cook sent for me and, looking out, I saw an amaz-ing sight. Mishka had watched her in the yard throwing corn to chickens and then catching one to kill. My bear had pondered the question. Now, copying her, he sat down and rubbed gravel between his paws, giving the effect of corn. The idiotic chickens ran up and started to peck. Immediately he caught one and made off. I had never the heart to reprimand him for this clever trick.

I gave two bears to General D. Radclyffe, who presented them to the London Zoo. They were called Tamara and Paul, after my children. In 1913 I gave one to Captain Stuart Richardson for his regiment, which collected money for the disabled, at Olympia.

Unfortunately Mishka got too sophisticated. When I was away the workmen started giving him vodka, which he consumed with unholy zeal. When drunk he got mad and danced wildly around, smashing things, so the agent had to have him locked up. Poor Mishka, he was just a little too human and came to a cruel end when the Bolsheviks swept through; they burnt him for being an aristocrat, along with my horses.

But apart from visits to country places I was tied to Petrograd and a feeling of futility and depression came over me, as it did over many young officers. The country life in Russia was the most glorious imaginable. I think the soil must be enchanted, for it is not just the haze of years that makes the trees, the flowers, the plains seem more beautiful than anywhere in the world. All Russians feel it, even the strange new generation who cross the border today, twenty years after the Revolution! But in grey, mysterious, introspective Petrograd, Peter's feverish young city that for two hundred years had stared towards the West without ever really taking anything of Europe unto itself, one became restive and dissatisfied. Russians do not belong to cities. Was there no other outlet for our pent-up energy than this pageantry of military service, this routine of balls and operas?

Foreigners came and were dazzled by the life we led, the splendour of the court, the wild, intoxicating nights on the Islands, the wonderful singing. How can one say in English that which is so easy to say in Russian, that we were simply trying to appease our souls? Englishmen when they want a good time *try* to live; we had no need to try, we simply did live intensely and naturally. A Russian never goes off with the jovial intent to "see life," he feels that he IS life.

Love played an important part in our existence. Russian officers lost their hearts with a violence that is unusual in placid England. Four or five of my companions in the Corps des Pages committed suicide over women and others were often on the verge of it (or said they were). In my own regiment one of the most charming, amusing fellows imaginable suddenly shot himself over someone else's mistress. Apparently he had wanted to leave the regiment and marry her and she wouldn't have anything to do with him. We none of us dreamed what was hidden by his gay manner until he blew his brains out.

These tragedies happened less often among women. The lovely things sang and talked about death but seldom took action, though on occasions fair deserted damsels were known to shoot themselves through the arm and then fall swooning, a trick which always brought to heel a panic-stricken swain.

I suppose we drank a certain amount, but we had enough energy without it. Young officers were sometimes encouraged to take too much champagne, as their superiors tested them out in this way. *In vino veritas!* One can judge a lot of a young man's character and self-control during one evening.

One amusing night in camp at Krasnoe Selo we all got a bit gay and started jumping out of a second-story window into the arms of the singers below, who caught us as in the gym. The party ended and most of us had gone to bed, when a cousin of mine woke up in some corner where he had been sleeping quietly, and staggered to the open window. Shouting to the non-existent singers to catch him, he leapt into space and landed heavily in a flower-bed beneath. An early gardener, amazed to see this apparition hurtling through the grey light of dawn, hurried off for help. The funny thing was that although the bed was studded with sticks for plants to creep up, in some odd way my cousin managed to fall between them and missed being spiked in half a dozen places!

Whenever Father left the country where he had outlets for his energy and came to Petrograd, he set the city humming and our house in a state of uproar. According to European standards he had very rough manners, but the Russians *en masse* admire brute force and his wild behaviour did not upset the servants, as it would have in other countries. About this time he organized his famous *Revue des Cocottes*. Hiring the Aquarium, the huge music-hall, for the evening, and a number of brass bands, he sent out invitations to all the cocottes of Petrograd and to a number of fellow officers. The Revue was held on military lines. Father and his friends stood on a platform while the ladies marched by and all the bands played. No-one who went has ever forgotten that night. As each damsel was given an expensive gift it was small wonder that the family fortunes began to wobble.

Life in the garrisons that were spread all over Russia was often very dull. In these far fortresses the officers had little to do except drink and gamble (unless they were lucky enough to be in a sporting district). Longing for excitement, they invented a game called Coo-coo, which became known all over Russia. I will describe it just to show the state of mind and nerve of the fellows who enjoyed playing it. Coo-coo was very simple. Two officers (after a good dinner) would toss for the pistol and go into a dark room. Then one would run around calling Coo-coo and hiding behind furniture, while the fellow with the pistol shot in the direction of the sound. After, say, three shots they would change over. This game sounds silly, but it was exciting enough at the time. The authorities took measures to stop Coo-coo, but it went on for years in spite of the number of deaths that resulted, in the same way that cockfighting did in England after it became illegal.

Coo-coo was just fun, however. Duels had to be fought seriously. Owing to very strict ideas of regimental honour, duels among officers were frequent and often fatal. All kinds of disputes were settled in this manner, but women were the most usual cause, as ladies always had to be extricated from any foolish scandal they had got themselves into, which was not always quite fair on the men who had to go out and fight.

One of my friends, Prince M——, always seemed to fall in love, most unfortunately, with married ladies. An affair with the wife of an absent naval officer got talked about. When the husband returned he challenged M—— to a pistol duel, and so did his younger brother. M—— fought both duels the same morning. It was arranged to shoot through a handkerchief (which, of course, made it more dangerous), starting 15 yards apart and advancing slowly, three shots allowed each man. M—— took on the two brothers in turn. One he wounded in the side and then blew the pistol out of the hand of the second. Then, himself unscathed, he returned home to breakfast. It paid Don Juans to be first-class shots as well! In this case the lady divorced her husband and married a new beau soon after—very feminine!

In spite of this gay and varied life I secretly rather yearned for a musical career; that being out of the question, I turned more and more to sport. My fellow officers shook off melancholy Russian moods with lovely women and champagne and mad gypsy songs; but this did not improve one's fitness and I was always in training for something.

Turning righteously away from consolations of debauch, I wistfully tried to soothe my longings by taking lessons in cornet-playing. I gave a little private concert and solemnly sat on a small gilt chair playing with puffed cheeks to a bevy of silent ladies. Needless to add, my wife remained upstairs that day.

But the cornet, though a purely masculine instrument, did not satisfy my desire for artistic expression, so I took up singing seriously. I had a strong, deep voice guaranteed to penetrate every wall and made good progress, though I could not resist trying it out on audiences.

My show piece, a touching little song called, "L'Ange et l'enfant," told the sad tale of an angel plucking a child from its cradle because it was too good for this earth. My father had composed the tune during a sentimental morning after. A friendly priest assured me it brought tears to his eyes, but my family soon taught me that my bass tones were unsuited to their drawing-rooms.

Song bringing no success, I took up equitation seriously. We naturally rode a great deal in the cavalry and the training of horses had absorbed me for some time. One of my geldings, an Irish bay named Toreador, seemed unteachable. In spite of all my work under ordinary instruction no good results could be obtained.

Some time previously an Englishman had come to Petrograd in a circus. His display of high-school work made such an impression that the Russian Imperial Government invited him to be "Ecuyer en Chef" at the Cavalry School. Several officers of my regiment, including Captain (now Field-Marshal) Mannerheim and my brother Alex, determined to train under this man, who invited us to his school to watch. We sat in a box listening carefully while he explained the technicalities of his work. He finished up with the most remarkable performance of high-school work we had ever witnessed. The beauty and ease of his horsemanship was incredible. A week later I started training Toreador under his direction. So it was that I became a pupil of the famous James Fillis and my life as a horseman began.

CHAPTER 8

Horsemanship & the Rome Embassy

A STOCKY LITTLE MAN with short bowed legs of great power and large sensitive hands, such was James Fillis. I worked with him every day for a year or more and saw him accomplish the most amazing feats, even making a horse canter backwards on three legs. He was a most intelligent teacher, always explaining details logically and clearly.

At the end of a year Toreador won the First-Class Imperial Prize and I proudly received a cup and personal congratulations from the Emperor.

After an unsatisfactory day I usually cheered myself up with Tzigane music. Gypsies could sing one out of the darkest mood. The famous Varia Panina often came from Moscow and her deep contralto still made men weep. She was fat and old and ugly but the exquisite, nerve-tearing timbre of her voice remained. Sad, passionate, angry and despairing by turn, when she sang Panina's youth returned and she moved one to a frenzy. No other gypsy woman ever reached those wild velvet depths of tone.

During the 1904 Revolution I met one of the most glamorous personalities of Petrograd, Nadejda, a beautiful blonde belonging to the curious, vibrant *demi-monde* of the City of White Nights. The result of a tragic romance between a General and a beauty of former days, she was a very child of love in character as well as by birth. Love was her whole existence, but she could be an intelligent, entertaining companion as well. Russian courtesans were known the world over for their beauty, but few writers have noted how unsordid they were. In no other capital have I seen the gay romantic type of *demi-mondaine*. In Paris they were different, over-dressed and uncultivated. In modern days one meets a new dull tin-can version with platinum hair. But the *hetairae* of Russia lived in a world apart, a hectic, tragic, unreal world in which there was no half measure, no place for old age, no possibility of marriage. Few of them came from the peasantry. I suppose they were mostly daughters of love or else middle-class women bored with middle-class life.

Somehow the light ladies of Petrograd were not just up for sale. During their brief, feverish careers they chose who they would. Certainly presents were lavished and diamonds were received as a matter of course, but they were not all out for money. In fact one often heard of a rich man deserted by his lady love who had fallen for some impecunious youth whom she wanted to "help."

Nadejda's life must have been one long round of presents, flowers and parties. She used to stroll along the Nevsky Prospect on fine days carelessly showing off her tall figure clad in the smartest of Paris gowns. Unending admiration and a trail of suitors gave her complete poise but never spoiled her childish sweetness. With care and thought she selected the man she wanted to love and let him know with disarming frankness.

"Kneeling lovers with outstretched arms weary me," she said quite unaffectedly as she reviewed the ceaseless struggle for her affections.

There was no better stimulant to romance than evenings in the innumerable gay restaurants of the Islands, and a drive home in a troika when dawn was whitening the crisp snow.

During the riots she had hot drinks for us after night pickets and she encouraged my equestrian career to the utmost. Enchanted by any attention, I worked desperately to impress her. When I started riding in shows the knowledge of her presence somewhere in the crowd, in a huge feathered hat, surrounded by flattering admirers made me go at the jumps as if life depended on it, and my horses (who always know these things) would also get excited and sometimes clear everything and sometimes meanly do the opposite! Nadejda's smiles spurred me to such lengths that Fillis insisted on giving me extra training, saying the result was his reward.

One summer my family took up the fashionable rage of going to spas and doing "cures." I spent dull days in Franzensbad while the ladies sipped and bathed and dieted till, overcome with boredom and longing for exercise, I went for a swim in the sulphur baths. After fifteen minutes I came out bright purple and sorely burnt, to be scolded and literally wrapped in cotton-wool for a week.

My work with Fillis ended when I was attached to the Embassy in Rome and I spent several months in that divine city. General Miller[1] was then Military Attaché and allowed me a great deal of free time, in which I seized the opportunity of taking fencing lessons with the world's greatest professors. I worked with Pecoraro, Columbetti and the famous Cavalier Musdashi.

The sensation of the season was a most beautiful society lady who took up ballet. Firmly convinced she was a prima ballerina, she gave a performance at which almost all Rome attended. In spite of her lovely face the lady could only walk about the stage on her *pointes* while men from the Russian ballet leapt around her and the audience shouted "Bis, bis" with tears streaming down their faces.

There was not much work to do at the Embassy. After the peace with Japan little seemed to be going on in the diplomatic world but inside Russia tremendous reforms were being made. The disorders of the First Revolution were slowly righted. The First Duma was summoned in 1906 in the Taurida Palace and many new fundamental laws passed. Mutual responsibility and

1. General Miller commanded White armies on the Northern Front, and after the disappearance of General Koutepoff, Head of the White Russians in Paris, took his place. He was himself kidnapped by the Soviet in October 1937 and has not been seen since.

redemption payments had been abolished, credit of the peasants' land bank increased and assistance was given to peasants with little land. Peasants were given equal privileges with other classes in entering Government services and educational establishments, but owing to their great dullness once they got off the land these privileges affected few. Other countries seldom realize the happy, animal-like stupidity of the Russian peasant, who sleeps on his stove all winter like a bear. The really important change lay in the peasant's new right to quit the village commune and own as his own property the land which he had cultivated and to which he had been entitled under the commune. This gave every peasant the pride of possession and a new impetus entered their lives. Now all this has been reversed again, and when a peasant protests against his plot being taken back into common property he is shot. We all found plenty to criticize in the old régime but the Tzar was working hard and approaching a constitutional monarchy.

Soon after arriving in Rome I went to see the Cavalry School at Tor di Quinto which had been reorganized by the famous Captain Caprilli. I watched the officers' performances cross-country with amazement. It was almost incredible that horses and riders should be able to negotiate such obstacles. The ease with which they went over the most dangerous jumps made me pause to consider. Fillis' training had helped me understand a great deal of the science of equitation, and in Russia I did not consider myself such a bad performer, but his whole interest really lay in light, free and beautiful high-school work. Although his training in no way interfered with a horse's usefulness in the country, he never obtained results such as these in the open. I talked with Captain Caprilli, who had had a severe struggle to work out and enforce his methods in Italy and had finally gained complete success. Over six feet tall, with a strong, lithe physique, Caprilli was one of the finest men imaginable. He told me: "There is no doubt that Fillis is the greatest master of high-school, but I do not agree with his principles for cross-country riding, as there is too much artificial balance. I try to develop the natural balance of the horse."

Returning to Rome, I asked the Italian War Office to be allowed a trial in the School. This being permitted, the Embassy saw me no more. "Horse fever" had got me again.

Fillis' advanced training had helped me obtain a certain success, but during this trial in the Cavalry School I realized I knew nothing about cross-country riding. The Cavalry School, with its terrific jumps, soon showed one up, but I loved it. Weary and bruised but ardent, I decided to ask the Tzar's permission to complete the eighteen-month course of the Italian Cavalry School.

CHAPTER 9

The Italian Cavalry School

Next autumn, after the main manœuvres in Petrograd, I was attached to the Italian Cavalry School by permission of the King of Italy. The Tzar agreed, knowing I could bring back useful knowledge to Russia. My elder brother Alex had finished the Petrograd Cavalry School and gone off to work at Saumur, the French Cavalry School, where he became a brilliant horseman.

In Turin we took Count Robillant's house (Via Gioto), and having installed my wife and children, I started the preliminary course at Pinerolo, which every young officer had to complete. Each morning at 5 A.M. I left home and motored forty kilometres to the Cavalry School, which stood in most beautiful country on the side of the pine-covered Alps. We started work at 6.30 A.M. and I never got home till evening, but what a thrilling time it was! When summer came we started work at 5 A.M., when dawn was just touching the far snow-covered Alps and the great mountains turned from white and purple to gold. We then finished at lunch time owing to the heat on the lower slopes.

Pinerolo got its name in A.D. 996 from the pine trees which surrounded it. I suppose it was just a village then, but it was to see centuries of fighting and struggle and have its own brilliant pages of history. In the sixteenth century Pinerolo fell under the rule of French kings. It was won back and retaken several times. During the longest period of French rule, which was 160 years, the conquerors fortified the town and turned the castle into a prison, where among others the famous "Iron Mask" was supposed to have been interred. In 1696 the French had to return Pinerolo to the Duke of Savoy, who destroyed all the citadels and bastions. Today Pinerolo lies calmly in its wonderful hills and the fortresses around the town are turned into lovely villas surrounded by vineyards and rose gardens. The streets are clean and picturesque and from the highest point there is a beautiful view of the Po valley and the soft green hills leading up to the great rocky mountains and kingly Monviso. The Cavalry School, with barracks, riding schools and hippodromes, adds a military appearance to the town.

The equestrian course is most strenuous. We worked five or six horses a day, as well as having physical drill, fencing, rifle practice and study of tactics. The officers were not supposed to leave Pinerolo during the week, but they had indefatigable energy and those possessing no cars often asked me for a lift to Turin for the night. A most uncomfortable incident occurred when the Commander of the Cavalry School unexpectedly went to Turin and asked me to motor him back in the morning. A certain young officer also had to return and be in his section at 6.30. Knowing the Commander's strictness, we were pretty nervous, but my chauffeur came to the rescue, dressed up my friend in a spare uniform and sat him on the box like a footman. In the back of the car I chatted away and noticed with amusement how careful the new footman was not to show his profile.

I had an Abyssinian valet at Turin, a tall, good-looking fellow who amused me vastly until I discovered he wore my civilian clothes whenever my back was turned. Hul dey Ess (son of Jesus) apparently had great temper and temperament. He tried to stab an Italian rival with an ordinary table knife, which simply bent and would not even penetrate his rival's clothes. Shouts of laughter were heard from the kitchen.

There were several fatal accidents at the Cavalry School while I was there, but I was lucky and only cracked my knees. I had

over a hundred falls and sometimes came home black and blue all
over, hardly able to move after being rolled on.

The sections often left the School and rode out in the glorious
country around Pinerolo. At first I could not believe these excur-
sions possible, but the horses became agile as mountain goats.
At an old *castello* we used to jump through the ruined windows
and go straight downhill. The horses crept and slid down small
cliffs and straight drops of 30 feet like cats, but there were many
uncomfortable moments, especially for anyone who suffered from
vertigo. One nasty time my horse fell and rolled with me down a
slope till stopped by a tree just above a precipice. The instructor
coldly commanded me to remount. I felt more inclined to cling
to the face of the mountain; I wanted to creep down the Alps on
my hands and knees.

Working from morning to night, the time went swiftly. Before
I realized it a year had fled by. The officers had an arrangement
whereby everyone paid 1 lira for each fall and at the end of the
course we gave amusing dinners with the money we had forfeited.
I had over 100 lira to my credit but we spent more on champagne! I got the Ottima Diploma for riding and also won a gold
medal for fencing.

Well pleased, I went off for a sun-baked holiday by the sea.

Next autumn I was transferred to Rome to finish the senior
course at Tor di Quinto. We lived in the Villa Rufo di Calabria
at Via Nomentana, with a fine view of the Alban Mountains.
The equestrian work naturally grew much more interesting. After
a year's gruelling groundwork one now revelled in practice and
advanced training.

Around the School were various hippodromes where we practised over natural jumps before going out into the Campagna
Romana. I had my first taste of Italian hunting. It was extraordinary to gallop through this ancient countryside with its mysterious broken statues and forgotten graves. As everyone knows, it is
stiff going, with high timber jumps and big stone walls, where a
mistake has dire results.

The work at Tor di Quinto though more advanced did not

seem as exhausting as at Pinerolo—perhaps because one now knew so much more—and as I was attached to the Embassy I went to many parties and had most interesting evenings. I found Italian society delightful and had a number of amusing friends of all nationalities. Among them were Commander Roger Keyes and his wife, who rode with the cool-headed brilliance that only British women with generations of fox-hunting behind them possess. The Commander rode with the courage that was later to be shown to the world when he became the hero of Zeebrugge. His talent, however, was stronger at blowing up harbours than manipulating horses across the Campagna Romana. I seem to remember numerous occasions when I helped his wife to bring him home with broken collar-bones, legs, arms and ribs in turn. Nevertheless a few weeks after any accident he reappeared with hounds as dauntless as ever.

Another character of the day, Count Pandolfi, Commander of Tor di Quinto, was a very smart rider and famous for the way he could take the biggest falls without dropping the monocle from his eye.

As the Russian Ambassador at that time was Mouravieff (ex-Minister for Justice), an extremely clever man, life at the Embassy could not have been more entertaining. Six months of hunting, riding and receptions flew by. At the end of the course I passed the highest examination with honours, and to celebrate, gave the party of my life at the Hotel Excelsior. The staff hasn't forgotten it yet. The whole Cavalry School came, officers, instructors, the Inspector-General, etc. It went on till 6 A.M. with everyone gay and happy. I found my last guests solemnly fishing sardines out of the piano, which had somehow become filled with champagne.

I was then transferred to a Cavalry regiment to finish in greater detail my knowledge of equitation. Before joining the regiment I had six months' leave and went back to Pinerolo to re-study the course from the Instructor's point of view. We lived in a small villa near the Cavalry School. During this time a delegation of officers was sent to Ireland to buy horses for the Italian Cavalry. I joined it and spent over a month travelling round visiting horse-dealers in that enchanting country I was to know some day so well.

We returned to Italy with some 200 horses—Ireland's best. Unfortunately my Italian sojourn ended there. I never joined the Cavalry regiment, for on returning to Pinerolo I found it necessary to fight a duel with an Italian officer. It was lucky that I had had years of training, for my opponent was an expert swordsman. According to Italian military law sabres were used. The contest proved no fun. I got cut over the eye and could not see, but at length I wounded my adversary severely and it was all over. I then dashed off to Switzerland, where my parents were staying, on the shores of Lake Geneva.

I installed my children at Montreux, which had become a sort of family meeting-ground. My parents lived in the Villa des Boyars, and my sister, Princess Chavchavadze, younger brothers and various nephews and nieces overflowed in several little houses around, and when that accommodation proved insufficient we took rooms in the Grand Hotel. The concierge still remembers the Rodzianko clan practising their diverse sports from early morning till nightfall.

CHAPTER 10

The King's Cup, Olympia

ON RETURNING TO Petrograd I was promoted to be A.D.C. to General Bezobrazov, Commander-in-Chief of the Guards. This meant that although attached to my own regiment I had to attend to the General as well as to my service. For several years I accompanied him to all inspections, parades and reviews of regiments in and around Petrograd. My social functions were also increased, as A.D.C.'s had to attend levées, balls and court functions. My duties entailed travelling around Russia with Bezobrazov and meeting many interesting foreigners as well as politicians, diplomats and Ministers.

I think I can truthfully say that having lived abroad I had learnt to see my country impartially as it really was.

General Bezobrazov was a real soldier, very military, disciplined and determined. Our friendship lasted until his death a few years ago.

Crowded and busy as the life was, Bezobrazov supported me in sporting events and gave me leave to ride in shows in Russia and abroad. Having the chance to carry on my work with horses, I managed in between other activities to organize evening classes in the Chevalier Guards' riding school and prepared a number of officers for International Competitions. The remainder of my spare time was spent training for fencing, skating and gymnastics.

Every summer we spent five months in camp at Krasnoe Selo. One night I got to bed late and was sleeping soundly when, before dawn, I was hurriedly awakened as the Grand Duke Nicolas, Commander-in-Chief, was making a sudden inspection. Blind with sleep I flurried about, getting tangled in my uniform and muttering imprecations. The men were too busy getting themselves ready to come to my assistance. In the faint grey light I pulled on a riding boot and then let out a yell, for something warm wriggled in the toe. "Help! help! Blast you all, help!" I shouted, for the boot was stuck and I could not get it off. I thought a rat would gnaw my toes away. Appealing loudly, I stumbled outside where officers and men were hurrying about in the cold half light. My roars brought attention, the boot was pulled off and out popped a terrified mouse!

That winter I was given three months' leave and travelled through Italy and Greece to Constantinople. From that city, as divine as it is dirty, we crossed the Black Sea to Batoum. A special train took us to Tiflis, the beautiful old Georgian capital where my brother-in-law Sasha Chavchavadze was A.D.C. to Count Woronzoff-Dashkoff, Viceroy of the Caucasus. The Chavchavadzes had been kings of Georgia until the eighteenth century, and Sasha, one of the most attractive men I ever saw, was a real Georgian type, tall, dark and good-looking, a fearless soldier and brilliant horseman. His father, Prince Z. Chavchavadze, had led several cavalry attacks during the Russo-Turkish war with startling bravery and become a well-known hero in his country.

Returning to Petrograd I did my service and trained for the forthcoming 1912 Horse Show at Olympia. Two of my pupils, Captain d'Exé of the Cuirassier Guards and Captain Ivanenko, accompanied me. We won a number of prizes, including the King Edward VII Cup. A curious thing happened on this occasion. The night before the competition I dreamed of jumping around the arena, winning and going up to the royal box to receive the Cup from King George. Next day my dream came true in every detail.

I had brought two horses from Russia and a third was sent straight from Italy. I had never seen this animal before, but it had been recommended to me by Captain Tappi, Instructor at the Italian Cavalry School. Knowing his understanding of horses and having been trained on the same principles, I trusted this horse enough to jump him for the King's Cup. Jenga only arrived at Olympia half an hour before the competition opened. I had just time to saddle him and ride out into the arena. He jumped like a bird and we won the Cup.

The excitement of our grooms over this triumph excelled anything seen in London. They went mad with delight, and one of them, a huge man with a beard, to the amazement of the English, flung his arms around me and kissed me as we rode into the yard to be photographed. Pictures appeared in the press next day with his barbaric face grinning in a corner.

We were invited to countless parties. Diaglieff's Ballet had taken London by storm that season and Russians were being fêted everywhere!

We returned to Moscow for the great celebrations to be held on the centenary of the war of 1812. On August 20 a great parade was held at Borodino of all the regiments that had taken part in the battle. Batteries were reconstructed, the same positions taken and the same large dark-faced ikon carried along in front of the massed troops. The Emperor, Empress, Tzarevitch and young Grand Duchesses were present, and many descendants of those who had fought in the battle, as well as the commanders of regiments. Most interesting of all were a number of old men who remembered the French invasion, an old peasant woman who had watched the battle, and the famous Sergeant-Major Voitiniuk who had fought and been wounded at Borodino at the age of twenty-two. He remembered the action clearly and, above all, enjoyed showing the spot where he fell.

The sun beat down all day just as it had on the two armies a century before, and when it set one thought of the 50,000 Russians who had been killed on that soil, and the 20,000 foreigners who must have wondered what they died for.

A tremendous feeling of patriotism was aroused by the reconstruction of that battle. The peasants and men were cheering all day—they even cheered the French Delegation!

Memorials were set up by various units on the places where their forebears had most distinguished themselves. My regiment, the Chevalier Guards, had done pretty well, charging in the thick of it and beating back Napoleon's infantry. This gave one a quite undeserved feeling of satisfaction.

I walked over the battlefield examining French and Russian positions. It was curiously exciting to visit the very hillocks where Napoleon and Kutuzov had been during the battle, able to see each other by telescope. And what did they think to get from that battle!

As Tolstoy says, the only results were to bring nearer the destruction of Moscow for the Russians and the destruction of their whole army for the French. Yet the genius Napoleon offered that battle and the shrewd veteran Kutuzov accepted.

Next spring I bought a new horse at a Military Show. He was a beautiful-looking Irish thoroughbred named "Macgillycuddy o' the Reeks" (a name most diversely pronounced by Russian tongues). He had the reputation of running away. I induced his owner, a Polish officer, to part with him and had two months to train him before Olympia. He proved a marvel, having intelligence and the most perfect structure.

June came and again the Russian officers had many successes at Olympia. I rode Macgillycuddy for the King's Cup and we won it a second time. President Poincaré was present, and I have still got a news clipping recording that my horse jumped so big in the last round that the great Frenchman threw his hat in the air with excitement!

I returned to Petrograd to finish manoeuvres and was invited by the American Horse Show Society to go over to New York and compete at Madison Square Gardens. Jenga and Macgillycuddy were put on a Russian steamer and sent across the Atlantic— owing to storms they took three weeks. I had only a fortnight in which to train them in New York. In spite of the rough passage the horses arrived in healthy condition, but soon showed signs of distress and could hardly stand when the time came. I was unable to discover the cause of their illness. I only dared jump Jenga, who won a couple of prizes.

In spite of this misfortune I had a wonderful time in New York. Even in Russia I had never seen such lavish hospitality and luxury. Although we had greater splendours yet our life was much simpler. The Americans made an art of party-giving. I will never forget a ball given by one of the Vanderbilts where the bar was made entirely of ice with a pool of champagne in the centre. I stayed at the Ambassadors Hotel, where my white Russian uniform seemed to create a sensation, and I am afraid I greatly enjoyed strolling through the foyer.

After a month of parties I returned to Russia where I won many more riding competitions and worked hard at my fencing. The excellent tuition I had had in Italy helped and I won the championship of Russia and also the Imperial Prize, a sword presented every year by the Tzar. For the third time I went to Olympia. Jenga, Macgillycuddy and Zorab between them were most successful and, as it was the third year in succession, we won the King Edward VII Cup outright and took it off to Russia.

I returned to Petrograd by sea and went to camp at Krasnoe Selo. The Chevalier Guards gave a dinner to celebrate the victory. The Grand Duke Michael, brother of the Tzar, presided, and ordered the King's Cup, which was placed in the middle of the table, to be filled with champagne. It held over two bottles, so I was naturally dismayed when the Grand Duke ordered me to stand up and drink it. Although furious I had to obey my Commanding Officer. Having protested in vain, I lifted the great cup to my lips. Dimly aware of the laughter and cheers of other officers, I began to drink.

"*Pey Dodna, Pey Dodna.*"

The drinking song that lasts till all is consumed grew farther and farther away. Before the cup was half empty I fell unconscious owing to the fumes. My party ended sadly, before it had really begun!

I think it was soon after this that Joffre came to Russia and big reviews were held at Krasnoe Selo. Anyway I remember dashing about on horseback all one stifling afternoon carrying messages in every direction for Bezobrazov and the Grand Duke Nicolas. The Emperor, with his usual kindness, called me: "Aren't you exhausted?"

My poor Emperor, if only he had been a little less kind, a little more brutal, a little less thoughtful for those around him, a little more ruthless for the sake of those he never saw, if only he had known how to fight and rule as well as he knew how to pray!

That summer was hot and oppressive. I did not trouble about the disquieting news in the papers, for the Olympic Games loomed ahead. They were to take place in Berlin and I was given leave to train specially as I wanted to win in five events. I was chosen to represent Russia in Riding, Skating, Fencing and Gymnastics, in which I had won many trophies. But my swimming was poor, so I went to Riga to practise, hoping to improve and enter for an event. For a warm heavenly fortnight I lived on the Baltic, swimming every day under expert instruction and browning in the sun.

One day as I was lying on the seashore a wire was brought me. Carelessly with wet fingers I opened it. The sun slipped behind a cloud and a cool wind seemed to creep up from the waves. Disappointed I changed into flannels and walked slowly home. The telegram recalled me to Petrograd immediately.

That gay, care-free life of sportsmanship had ended for ever. It was July 1914.

PART II

The War

To read many modern writers one would suppose that the war came by itself, and that no person in authority ever thought of such a wicked thing . . . The theory that it all happened by itself, that Germany carelessly gave Austria a blank cheque to correct Serbia, that Russia was indignant at the spectacle, that Germany was alarmed because Russia mobilized, that France and England did not tell Germany in time that she would fight, that all Berchtold wanted was his little private war with Serbia, that all the Kaiser wanted was a diplomatic triumph . . . all these cases find ample documentary support. Still certain stark facts which no elaboration can veil stand forth for all time.

—Winston Churchill, *The Eastern Front*

CHAPTER 11

Russia Mobilizes

BEFORE I REACHED Petrograd rumours of mobilization spread like wildfire over the country. Sitting in the train I reflected on the situation. We knew the German mobilization plans had been drafted in March, but this summer, after a lot of discussions, the leaders of the various countries had gone off on holiday, the Kaiser to the Baltic, Poincaré to Cronstadt. Now in a hot compartment rumbling northwards it suddenly seemed that the tension of the last six months made it obvious war might be declared at any minute. In the words of Berchtold (whom I remembered so clearly smiling over the champagne at many diplomatic dinners), Sarajevo was to be made the occasion for Austria's reckoning with Serbia. The Austrian Ultimatum to Serbia seemed grave, but such crises had occurred before and had passed. We could not know the extent to which the Kaiser had backed Austria, but Sazonoff, our Minister for Foreign Affairs, must have known very well that German mobilization meant war. Everything concerning German mobilization plans were known to France and Russia. Once Germany began to mobilize as reply to Russian mobilization, Sazonoff could not have believed a European war was to be averted.

As long as possible the Tzar struggled against war. During four hectic days he and the Kaiser exchanged brotherly telegrams. But while "Nicky" and "Willy" sent their long cousinly wires, preparations for mobilization continued.

Night fell as the train rattled northwards, and staring out at the darkening forests a curious, oppressive excitement crept over me. If it came to a scrap we knew the Russian Army had improved in every way. Plans for strategic railways to the western border were developing, but unready. Yet it could not be another 1904. We had changed since then. We were ready to fight, full of courage, sure of ourselves.

Arriving at Petrograd in the morning of July 27, the day after Serbia submitted to the Ultimatum, I found a city seething with excitement. As in Vienna, Berlin, London and Paris, everyone rushed around discussing the possibility of war.

I reported straightway to my General, Bezobrazov, Commander of the Guards. He told me to be ready for any emergency but not to say a word, as official mobilization was not yet declared. Driving back to my mother's house, I noticed crowds in the streets, gesticulating and talking. With night it became difficult to maintain order. Drunken rabbles had taken to giving "patriotic demonstrations" outside the Austrian Embassy.

On July 28 the Kaiser, given Serbia's submissive reply, thought a quiet victory had been accomplished, but at that very moment Berchtold was declaring war on Serbia. Next day Belgrade was bombarded and the fever spread. The German Ambassador declared to Sazonoff that if Russia continued to prepare for mobilization Germany would be forced to attack.

The desperate personal telegrams of Tzar and Kaiser were of no avail. On July 30 Nicolas II having striven his utmost for peace was forced by Samsonov and the military authorities to sign a ukase of General Mobilization. An hour later the military centres were informed.

On August 1 Germany declared war on Russia and then on France. And so it happened. The hurricane descended and swept our world away. One can search in vain for sufficient reason. On the surface it happened because Berchtold was determined to have his war with Serbia, and the Kaiser had encouraged them, know-

ing the result must arouse Russia. I suppose a deeper reason lay
in unequal distribution of world necessities and inadequate peace
efforts between diplomats, who, incidentally, did not have to fight.

I remember the quiet, empty rooms in my mother's house that
evening of July 30. I was alone there and most of the servants
on holiday. A house deserted for the summer holidays takes on
a mysterious, unfamiliar quality. Wandering around the silent
library I was idly looking for some book when the telephone summoned me to General Bezobrazov. General mobilization had
been declared, and he told me to report immediately. Early next
morning, a cog in the vast machine just set in motion, I started
mobilizing men, horses and motorcars. I do not remember being
able to lie down or sleep for three days. I ate while working.

During the ten hectic days before leaving for the front, the
peaceful city suddenly became a shouting tumult with manifesta-
tions at every turning. Crowds surged down the streets, all elated,
excited, busy. Like hysterical ants they ran hither and thither in
unaccustomed activity. The shops were packed with people buying equipment for the front.

Cheering mobs stood nightly in front of the French and British Embassies. On August 3, the night before England declared
war on Germany, a crowd went to the British Embassy, shouting for the Ambassador, Sir George Buchanan, and demanding
that England should join the Allies. I was passing at the time on
one of those interminable searches for motorcars, and the crowd,
seeing an officer, asked me to induce Sir George to appear. He
was a friend of mine, so I went in and persuaded him to come
out on the balcony. Of course he could not make a speech as
they wanted, but the crowd interpreted his appearance as they
wished and disappeared, cheering lustily. What did they know
about politics, any of them? What did they know about the rights
or wrongs of the war they hailed? Why did they scream for England to join? Looking back from this new hectic time of dictatorship, one sees how ridiculous and how weak is the mind of
the masses. Then, as now, they think what their newspapers told
them to think. Whatever they read most often in the biggest type

is what nations believe. The masses become indignant, hysterical or conceited, according to the propaganda handed out to them. A few years of anti-war books and films have not changed the human mind, they have simply led to pacifists wanting to exterminate non-pacifists. Peace is now the excuse for war. The last war did not really lead to any new discoveries about the beastliness of fighting. It has always been unpleasant to die and suffer physically. Men have known that for centuries. Last time it was on a bigger scale and less picturesque than previously. That was the only difference. Next time it will be bigger still but not quite so ugly, as aeroplanes are more attractive than tanks.

General Bezobrazov advised me to send for my children from Usviat. They just got through in time as the Vitbsk railway was closed except for military purposes.

Now that war was actually declared, a curious exultation held the Russian masses. Foreigners in Petrograd at the time remarked at the orderliness of the crowds and the complete absence of drunkenness. It was as if we were going to the Crusades. The war seemed popular with every class. Even the strikers returned to work and a quarter of a million people stood in the Palace Square while the Tzar swore in the words Alexander I had used during the Napoleonic invasion. He would "never make peace while an enemy remained on Russian soil." All Russia shouted.

Will I ever forget those hot, feverish days at the beginning of the war? The wild, terrible excitement, the flushed, elated faces of young officers longing to fight, the woebegone anxiety of my two younger brothers so afraid of "missing it"? In the eyes of some women, perhaps, lurked misgiving, but the crowds surged through the streets madly enthusiastic. All night we heard them till the warm purple sky seemed to catch and hold their cheers.

Still I can hear the thunderous hymn that was sung before Borodino. Thousands of voices took it up all over the city and through the cloud of sound one could hear the feet of soldiers marching. Is it believable they sang and shouted for that war?— the war that was to mean death to most of them and, for those who survived, bondage or exile?

CHAPTER 12

The Grim Reality

> History will recognize the intensely loyal efforts made
> by the Tzar and his generals to make their onfall with
> the greatest possible strength. —Winston Churchill

FIFTY MILLION RUSSIANS were involved by mobilization orders.
My children went out with their governess to spend their
pocket-money on a little ikon that I was always to carry at the
front. Flushed and elated they presented the gift amid blessings
and farewells. From time immemorial children have enjoyed the
proud moment when "Papa goes to war." I went off with General
Bezobrazov to Warsaw, where the Guards united near the fortress
of Novogeorgievsk. On the vast front where Russia faced her enemies the Guards would be used carefully, transported from place
to place for the most important attacks.

While to the south the Austrian cavalry, attacking in brilliant
red and blue uniforms, were driven back easily, the Germans in
the north proved a more difficult matter.

We found our troops longing to fight. General Bezobrazov,
inspecting the men daily, was deluged with questions as to when
they would see action. The Guards Cavalry was advancing with
General Rennen-kamf to the north and the victory of Gumbin-

nen filled us with jealousy as well as joy. The war was being won
without us!

Meanwhile France shouted for help and the original Russian
plan to attack only the Austrians and fight the Germans on the
defensive was changed to help our allies in the West. We were to
save Paris by attacking violently. The Grand Duke Nicolas, the
fine soldier we all loved and trusted, gave the orders to advance—
and proud, hungry, unorganized Russia advanced.

In the beautiful old city of Warsaw spirits were high. There is
no stimulant like the beginning of war. In spite of crowds of military and Red Cross, civilian life went on as usual, more romantic, more intense. The population had increased tremendously
as, apart from officials, hundreds of country folk had flocked to
the town and every hotel was overflowing. A feeling of confident
expectancy filled the air as if something wonderful must happen
and all day the sun blazed down on the gaily thronged avenues.

Among officers one could detect a curious tenseness. We wanted
danger and seethed inwardly when others were sent to scenes of action. When a desirable woman comes into the presence of a group
of men, the same rather strained atmosphere arises. I had often
noticed the effect in Petrograd. We who had been good comrades
ten minutes before would stiffen, try to show off, watch peevishly
another's success. One could not really call it jealousy; like a whiff
of perfume it entered with a feminine presence and faded with her
departure.

And war drifted in like a strange new woman, more thrilling, more aloof. We sighed for her touch, we dreamt of glory in
her arms. Old men and wise might gaze on dispassionately, but
for months we were infatuated with her glamour. It takes years
to learn what war really is and what she leads to. And some men
still love her when they know. It is no good trying to teach that
to our sons. War, like love, is an experience that each generation
must learn for itself.

The Guards headquarters were fixed at the Bristol Hotel and
we motored to and from the regiments outside the city. The
first new war-song had been invented and, like "Tipperary" in

England, one heard it everywhere, sung in the streets, whistled, hummed. "As we passed Warsaw's bridges the girls threw flowers" went the words.

After a few days our headquarters were moved to Novogeorgievsk. There the Guards Infantry united and General Bezobrazov made endless inspections. During those days of concentrated work one did not have time to think.

From Novogeorgievsk I was sent out to motor to the northern front and tell Samsonov to keep in strict contact with us as the Guards Infantry was intended to support him. Before I arrived at Mlava, however, a counter order arrived to move the Guards back from Novogeorgievsk to Warsaw.

For a few days I stayed in the Bristol Hotel with General Bezobrazov while the Guard Corps were transferred to the southern Lublin front, where they were to join the 4th Army and roll up the Austrian left.

On August 29 Lieut.-Colonel Alfred Knox, British Liaison Officer, dined with us. I remember General Bezobrazov telling him how the young men of the Guards were thirsting to fight— 30,000 men of fine calibre. We were all in good spirits, thinking the war would soon be over, longing to meet the enemy. For days Bezobrazov had been pestered by officers and men all asking the same question: when would they see the Germans and have a fight?

"Wait, you'll get plenty," he answered with a smile. He reserved encouragement for times of action when his words were needed. Russian optimism did as much harm as our equally profound pessimism. We underrated difficulties and would then suddenly lose heart, whereas the Germans always advanced with the same detailed precautions.

The victory of Gumbinnen had raised our hopes, but as we sat there in the busy hotel, smoking a hasty cigarette and talking of "the end," the battle of Tannenberg had taken place. Samsonov's 2nd Army had been annihilated. Aimless, hungry and confused, worn out by days of marching, thousands of Russians, knowing themselves surrounded in a great forest, laid down their rifles.

Knox had visited General Samsonov the day before and had just returned through Neidenberg in time.

That very evening the beaten leader blew his brains out in the woods, leaving the remnant of his men to make pitiful attempts at escape while desperate young officers shot themselves. All this we were not to know for weeks. Little recking, we ate a good supper and went to our clean hotel beds.

Next day I accompanied General Bezobrazov to Lublin with the Guards. There I found my charger, Macgillycuddy, waiting for me and a smaller horse to undertake the menial task of carrying my kit. As General Bezobrazov's A.D.C. I guessed I would be constantly on the move and had therefore made careful arrangements as to kit. It seemed just as easy to be comfortable as otherwise, and so I had sent for a waterproof canvas bed and plenty of silk underclothes (which lice dislike!). At first my silken underwear and sleeping-bag caused mirth, but when I proved the only one who always had a dry bed, the jeers of fellow officers turned to envy.

The arrival of the Guards on the line Lublin–Kholm enabled Russia to take the offensive against the Austrians. Owing to the already strained railways we had difficulty getting there, however. Seven miles from Kholm our train ran into what resembled a large-scale modern traffic block. Incompetent officials had allowed a number of trains to get muddled up and lines were blocked in all directions. Hours passed and we could get neither forward nor back. Worst of all, General Bezobrazov could not get in touch with the General Staff. He called me and asked if it were not possible to get some of the horses out. Their vans were on a kind of viaduct with a steep bank leading straight down from the track.

Here Macgillycuddy would show his stuff! We opened the van door, led him to look down for himself and gave him a little vocal encouragement. "Heavens!" he seemed to think, "worse than my first bank in Ireland." Then like a cat he leaped down and slid to safety. The troops clapped. No other horse there would have done it, and with justifiable pride I saddled him and cantered off to headquarters. If there was a St. George's cross for animals he would have won it that day.

The Guards went into battle with delight and worked to perfection in spite of great losses.

Early one morning I rode over a hill which the famous Pavlovski Regiment of the Guards had charged and taken the previous day. The summer sun was gilding grass still wet with dew, a frightened bird flew from a tree when I passed, but, listening, one heard no song as is usual at that hour. Silence did not become this glittering morn. The slope of the hill I rode up was strewn with figures all facing one way and with a terrible likeness between them, as if a thousand brothers lay dead together. Paul I was well known for his turned-up nose, and, since he founded the regiment over one hundred years ago, the men selected all had *retroussé* noses. Courageous and faithful as lions they lay on the ground, fine, strong men all over 6 foot; how proud they had been of their noses! I don't know why that detail made one's heart ache. The men had always thought it such fun to qualify for the Pavlovski Regiment; some of them looked perky still. I could not bear to look at them, death fitted those brave pug faces so awkwardly.

War is full of curious sights and accidents. A line of Russian soldiers was attacking a hill, advancing as usual, and dropping flat every few yards. Shells were coming over the top of the hill and bursting all around. A man ran ahead and dropped; suddenly his coat was flat on the ground as if the body of its wearer had vanished by magic. One minute there was a man, the next minute only clothes. Later we discovered his head had been hit by a shell which carried his body right away without touching his coat.

Later on the enemy were attacking Lomja by air. As the aeroplanes appeared everyone sought shelter and one soldier hid in a rain-water barrel, near a house. By ill chance a bomb fell straight into the barrel, leaving nothing of it or its contents.

During the three weeks' battle of Lemberg the Austrian front was driven back 150 miles. Hundreds of thousands were slain and the Russians showed their mettle, fighting all day and sleeping on the ground at night. The Austrian Army wavered and broke in three weeks, the cry of "Kosaken kommen" being enough to put whole regiments to flight!

"Hundreds of thousands were slain"; how casually one reads those words in the histories of war, but it is impossible to realize what they actually mean. Before seeing a battlefield you imagine vaguely what fighting entails, but no writer has ever described the reality. One's brain becomes numb. Afterwards you look back as on a dream and remember queer details, but at the time one walks among the dead and dying completely unmoved because feelings have just got to be pushed away. Besides, one is soon too tired for horror or fear or even sorrow.

When I went into the captured enemy lines the same sights met my eyes. Everywhere bodies lying, and what hate had been conjured up by the warmongers speedily faded. One cannot hate men who die gallantly. Soldiers do not hate, only those who stay at home and talk.

Among the first killed was Bibikov, a young Lancer of the Guard and a brilliant horseman. We had wrestled together at the Corps des Pages, and when I returned from Italy he became one of my best pupils. Apart from jumping competitions he won many races, and the day before his death we sat together by a campfire discussing that gay youth which suddenly seemed so far off. He was killed in a Cavalry charge against a wood. General Mannerheim, Commander of his Brigade, was heartbroken. We found Bibikov early next morning lying in the wood. His badges and shoulder-straps had been cut off by the enemy to find out what regiments were in the district. His white handsome face looked so young! The funeral service was held in a stable full of horses—the congregation he would have chosen.

How quickly the best young fellows seemed to get wiped out, people like myself being left. The depression caused by the deaths of one's friends wore off, leaving one devoid of feeling or desire except to obey orders and do one's job well, so that the slaughter might stop soon.

Even Macgillycuddy, pampered, temperamental beauty that he was, grew accustomed to the sight and smell of corpses. In the end he took war as calmly as he had taken applause at Olympia.

One evening during the advance, the Guards took a village towards dusk. Fighting had been heavy and the trenches were piled high with dead of both sides mostly killed hand to hand with bayonets. In an endless diversity of positions they lay. Only death could arrange such strange patterns of limbs without repetition. Some stiff, some twisted, some still breathing, the long lines of bodies stretched in every direction. And no man lay the same. Kindly night descended.

Stumbling into a large barn, my batman and I fed and watered the horses as best we could, and in the darkness lay down to heavy slumber. Towards dawn I awoke, surprised to find a boot in my face, but too tired to investigate. When morning arrived I sat up to see a leg sticking out of the straw beside me. I pulled, and a dead Austrian rolled out of his last hiding-place. Wounded, he had crept into the straw and died beside me during the night. Unenchanted by this strange bed-fellow, I saddled the horses and left him there with a curious, almost childish smile on his face.

Some days later I noticed our tea smelt odd and went to investigate the water used. My batman showed me an innocent-looking brook. Five minutes upstream, however, I found several rotting corpses and that of a horse, which had hardly improved our beverage.

The Austrian officers captured were usually invited to breakfast in our mess. We were giving the poor devils coffee and cigarettes when one came up with a smile:

"Remember two months ago?" he asked.

I stared back unrecognizingly.

"Aren't you the Rodzianko I saw winning the King's Cup at Olympia this year?"

"Yes." We stared at each other and laughed. In the distant golden world of two months ago we had met. I remembered him, a smart young officer "mad keen" on riding, who never missed an event at Olympia.

"The horse I rode is with me now," I told him, and for half an hour we talked the "shop" of horsemen, as if no war had come between us.

The Austrians retreated *en masse* and thousands of prisoners were taken. Carts of wounded jolted all day towards Lublin and many died silently on those rough roads. We had a great deal of hand-to-hand fighting. I came on two figures leaning together as if dancing. A Russian and an Austrian with each other's bayonets through their middles, they had died at the same moment staring into each other's faces, their fingers clutching the butt ends of their guns.

One evening riding back to headquarters I passed a wood we had taken in close fighting. The dead lay in heaps ten deep with hundreds of wounded still moving. Soft evening light fell through the trees and the effect was of a huge pile of fish that has been out of water some time but still breathes and flaps for life. Their gasping cries made a great sigh in the forest. Alone I could do nothing to help. The sight was too appalling to be tragic and I could but ride on.

Yet bitter fighting did not seem to alter the kindly Russian nature. Colonel Knox noticed how good our men were to their prisoners, often giving up cigarettes and bread they needed themselves. War destroys the pettiness in human nature. All the depths of unselfishness and cruelty are revealed.

It is interesting to note that at this time Conrad, the Austrian C.-in-C., wrote that his troops were "fighting as gallantly as the Germans who are engaged not against Russians but only against Frenchmen!"

With the war, alcohol was suddenly banned throughout Russia. In other countries the Russians' liking for vodka is regarded as a joke, but although the raw liquid did great harm to the peasants and might have had a bad effect on soldiers already over-excited by war, this sudden law meant that the fellows had nothing to warm themselves up with during the cold or before a charge and immediately led to a great deal of secret drinking. Whenever the chance occurred wine was looted and stolen. How different the

Cossacks were from my brother-in-law's Georgians. Alexander Chavchavadze commanded the "Wild Squadrons," the Circassian Horse Regiment, and these fearless warriors, bred in the mountains, proud and disciplined, never drank owing to their religion, and scorned the debauchery of their Russian brothers.

There was a fine young Don Cossack in the Guards, a giant, very handsome and *naïf*. He got drunk on strong Hungarian Tokai plundered from a château. When reprimanded he did not recognize the Commandant of the camp and tried to attack him. He did not realize his offence until, waking up in a cell, he found himself in for a court-marshal. He was condemned to be shot for breach of discipline.

I happened to be sent by General Bezobrazov to inspect the prisoners in the cellars of the château and came across this fellow.

"Gritzko, what on earth got you here?"

He told me.

"Sir, I can't remember anything, only don't let my family know I was shot for this. Let them think I was killed in battle. I could not bring such shame to my father." I looked up at this great child with bobbed curly hair. What a specimen!

I resolved to try to get him sent to the front lines where he could be of some use and die honourably.

Going to General Bezobrazov I used my utmost diplomacy, but to no avail.

"Discipline has got to be upheld. I cannot make exceptions."

I insisted, but although the General listened to my points he dismissed me impatiently:

"Don't go on, Paul. There is nothing to be done."

But just as I left the room thinking my arguments had failed, he called, "Come back. I'll sign your damn petition and have him sent to the front line."

I broke the news to Gritzko myself. Overcome with joy he tried to kneel and kiss my hand. I had saved not his life but his honour, which to a Cossack meant far more.

Delighted to get to the front lines he covered himself with glory. His bravery was that of an inspired man. He received several decorations and eventually was killed, as he wished to be, on the battlefield.

During the advance we captured a great deal of German and Austrian transport. As they had to retreat by a single road under constant shell-fire their casualties became enormous. Broken carts, dead men and horses lined the road. Surrounded by bog and forest they could not leave that single track. We could hardly collect our own wounded, far less stop for abandoned Austrians. All day one rode along this highway of devastation, the shy autumn sun casting a soft light on heaps of dead and blackened villages. We rode, we reconnoitred, we attacked, but we did not look at the debris of the enemy. Who wants to see smashed guns and mangled bodies? Except for one unusual incident I remember few details. Early one morning we trotted past a big German lying on the ground, face down, with a head wound and seemingly dead except that one arm ceaselessly flicked away flies from his ear. Next day we returned along the same road and he lay in exactly the same position, his hand still flicking. How long this strange nervous spasm lasted I shall never know, but the incident remained in my mind.

Otherwise one thought only of ammunition, food, saddles, horses' backs and the paraphernalia of war. On each side of the ghastly roads we travelled lay black Polish bog, and the forests beyond shimmered with silver birch. Slender silver trunks and vivid gold leaves, golden as fire in the darkness of other trees, mockingly beautiful.

So the first round ended with the Austrian retreat, and about the middle of September came a pause on all fronts. Our hearts still beat for the glory of war though we were sickened by the reality.

CHAPTER 13

War in the Snow

If the Russian Cavalry did not attain in the war the results that were hoped from its vast numerical superiority over the enemy cavalry, it was not the fault of the trooper or of his officers up to the rank of Squadron Leader. —General Knox, *With the Russian Army*

As a result of events on the Western Front, by autumn the whole burden of war lay on Russia's shoulders. The Allies, realizing the terrible crisis our country must pass through trying to hold a front without munitions, tried to keep up the conviction that war must be continued.

In October the Russian Armies were regrouped and the second round began. While Hindenberg started his great offensive against Warsaw the Grand Duke Nicolas planned a Russian advance into Germany. Says Hindenberg: "It was unquestionably a great plan of the Grand Duke, indeed the greatest I had known."

The two offensives began independently but Russian plans were revealed to the enemy by wireless. The Germans advanced, fighting brilliantly, and we soon knew they were harder mettle than the Austrians. When they had to retreat we found they had made detailed preparations. Their organization was superb. When we Russians advanced even fifty miles our men were shouting they had reached Berlin, and the officers were discussing Christmas plans when "the War is sure to be over." Only Germans could creep relentlessly forward, planning as they did how to retire if necessary.

I had been sent to the south to collect machine guns when the Guard Rifle Brigade was attacked on October 4 and lost nearly 9000 men at Opatov. On approaching Anapol I discovered the guns I sought were the other side of the Vistula and the Germans were approaching pretty near. Small steamers still crossed the river and I managed to cross with my car. Having motored off to a picket I discovered where the guns were, a mile or so away, and sent them back to the awaiting steamer. We got them all on a barge to be towed behind. The German guns were getting nearer and the steamer had to escape upstream to Warsaw. We moved off hurriedly and the rope pulling the barge caught me in the chest, knocking me fully equipped into the water. My heavy coat, riding boots, revolvers and sword did not make a good swimming costume and the current was strong. After a few strokes I began to sink in the icy swirl. All the usual thoughts of the drowning ran through my head, and what a foolish end it seemed to be! I had almost lost consciousness when the car mechanic saw my splashes, jumped in and somehow got a rope around me.

Having given up hope it was almost unpleasant to come back to life and find myself frozen and soaked and uncomfortably full of river water. Shivering in an icy wind I struggled to the engine-room, the only warm place on that little ship. There I stripped and spent two warm hours while my clothes dried. I did not particularly want to report this exploit but had to, so that my brave rescuer should get a decoration.

Rain and wind swept over Poland, turning the roads to liquid mud and causing great privations to the armies. We did not mind, thinking that Russians could stand physical hardship better than town-bred Germans.

When the Guard Corps moved to the fortress of Ivangorod, General Bezobrazov placed in my charge Lieut.-Colonel Knox, the British Liaison Officer, whom I had known as Military Attaché in Petrograd. While he visited our front I was to show him round but keep him as much as possible out of danger. Knowing as much as he did about Russia, he would have been a big prize to the enemy. Unfortunately my charge proved as rash as he was valuable, and my job became very difficult. The centre of the firing-line held an incomprehensible attraction and he constantly led me into the most uncomfortable positions.

The very day of his arrival a cannonade started near by. We walked across the bridge over the Vistula and watched enemy shells bursting about three versts away. Knox spoke of his great admiration for the Russian Guardsman: "If only he had regular rations he would be hard to beat."

Every day we covered long distances, visiting various corps, and generally starting at dawn. Sometimes we found the Staff in a hovel, sometimes in a palace, such as that of Prince Czartoriskis, built on the plan of Fontainebleau with an avenue several miles long.

The Russian attack started near Ivangorod. Knox and I rode out to watch. As we approached the front lines from behind a hill, stretchers and wounded poured past us. Soon we were in range of rifle bullets and, fearing our horses might get hit, dismounted and left them with the orderly. Amid what seemed a hail of bullets we crept on to the top of the hill. I remonstrated in vain. "Listen, Flurry, I have strict orders to TAKE CARE of you. And anyhow I should never come here on my own. What's the good of getting killed for nothing?"

"Come on, old boy; let's see what's going on."

I could guess quite well what was "going on," but the Irishman must get to the top of the hill with bombs bursting in all directions.

One could see nothing.

"How about lunch?" asked Knox brightly, as if he had discovered the most delightful place for a picnic. Sourly I answered I did not feel like enjoying a meal.

"Bet it takes more than this to reduce *your* appetite," was the heartless reply, and sitting on a large stone we munched sandwiches while barrage-fire increased.

Afraid our horses would be killed, I insisted on leaving. "Give me a match for my pipe," he answered. But we started back. We had got a hundred yards away when a shell burst on the stone we had been sitting on! Even this did not shake my friend.

"But your life is valuable," I pleaded. "You are a fool to go under fire when it's not your job."

"But I want to see . . ."

"Well, if you carry on you won't see anything. And I hate it."

"Poor Nurse," he teased.

We argued amidst shell-fire the whole way back.

One evening we arrived at the village of Zvolen an hour after the Austrians had evacuated. The place was full of typhoid. Entering the good-sized Catholic Church we found it full of Austrian wounded. One could hardly walk they were so closely packed. They lay on straw on the stone floor with no-one to dress their wounds or give them water. They had been without food for three days. Many were dead and others dying, painfully, pathetically before our eyes. The ghastly, sickening smell of mouldering flesh and excrement choked one. Few of them moved when we came in, but their eyes followed us hopefully, and in the soft moaning there were whispers of "Wasser, wasser."

We immediately made some tea and went around with cigarettes and chocolate for those who could swallow. When my soldiers arrived they took one look at the suffering, starving figures strewn over the cold floor and offered at once to give up all their bread as "We will get more to-morrow." There was nothing more we could do for these pathetic remnants abandoned by retreating regiments. They all had something to eat or drink but their wounds could not be dressed. We left them in the darkness with only the great altar cross to give them comfort and watch over their torn bodies with its sad, compassionate figure.

On the outskirts of the village I entered a hut; a frightful stink filled the darkness. Then a weak voice called. I found two Austri-

ans badly wounded who had been lying four days without food
or water, unable to move. The smell came from the bodies of two
comrades who had died beside them.

Knox and I shared a room at the priest's house. "Good lor',
we're actually going to have fresh air," said he as I flung open our
bedroom window. One felt the foetid church air sticking to one's
lungs.

After a stand-up breakfast next day we rode out to visit the
Staff of the First Division of the Guard. While we were there a
report came in that the body of a drummer of the Preobrajensky
Regiment had been found mutilated by the Austrians. We rode
on to the village where he was being buried. The drummer's company, all picked men over 6 foot, were drawn up in a fir wood.
The priest chanted the service over the open grave and in the
dusk it was a majestical ceremony.

On October 26 the Germans evacuated Radom and soon we
heard they were retreating from Poland. The priests of various
small villages we rode through told us of officer prisoners made
to drag guns.

One bitterly cold day Knox and I rode to Ilja, a charming little old village with a tenth-century castle. We spent the night
as usual at the priest's house. He welcomed us with open arms
for the Germans had occupied this village for four weeks and
robbed everyone, even the General paying with worthless marks.
A woman told me that whenever the Germans occupied a village
they collected the women and picked out the best ones for the
officers. Rape is too wild a word for the disciplined, organized
"love"-making that followed. Russians were probably much worse
when they got mad but I do not think we did such things in cold
blood. It would not have amused us.

On the last day of October I managed to get off to Warsaw
to see about some motor repairs. Knox accompanied me to get
his dispatch through to Petrograd. We arrived late at night in
a wild snowstorm. All the way Knox chaffed me because I was
so anxious to see my wife, and to my dismay an account of this
trip appeared when his war diary was published describing him-

self "given furiously to thought" about military matters while I planned frivolities and cursed the chauffeur's slowness. Thirty miles out of Warsaw we saw a huge body of artillery. An officer told us they were off to Turkey!

While in Warsaw my orderly stupidly allowed my horses to fight and lame each other. Macgillycuddy had taken a dislike to his less well-bred companion and lashed out the moment he got the chance.

When I got back to the front the weather was bitterly cold. I rode my orderly's horse until he went lame. The horses had to have *shipi* nails screwed onto their shoes to keep them from slipping.

The German offensive opened in north Poland. Russia suffered terribly from our Government's peace-time policy of not building railways "on strategical grounds" to the front. The theatre was prepared for a defensive war and we had been fighting an offensive. Still, in spite of the primitive mechanical efficiency of our Army, the enemy have paid deep tribute to "the Grand Duke's great knowledge of military art."

Owing to the cold, the men began to suffer terribly in the trenches, but they thought the enemy would suffer more.

We knew our situation was not brilliant. There was general anxiety about the shortage of ammunition, which was especially serious in the 2nd Guard Division. On November 19 the Division had only 180 rounds per rifle left, and the Guards had come to a standstill. In the terrific frost many men froze to death. Reinforcements arrived to replace the heavy losses but were helpless without ammunition.

Having run out of shells and bullets and knowing the Germans were ready to attack was no fun. At the village of Stsiborjitse we heard the ammunition train had been lost somewhere on the way to the front. General Bezobrazov summoned me. I could see he was seriously worried.

"Look here, Paul, the situation is pretty bad. The ammunition train has got stuck no-one knows where. Here we are at S——. You must ride to Army headquarters at Mehov and from there get a car to the nearest station. You have full authority to commandeer all motors, horses, carts and vehicles of any description from the Guard Corps. I give you *carte blanche* and only trust you will get the ammunition to the regiments by noon tomorrow. Further arrangements I leave entirely to you. It will be difficult but I trust you. Get off as quickly as possible and good luck."

I saluted and went to my room rather worried. What responsibility and what a job to find a probably non-existent munitions train on a frozen, disorganized front of hundreds of miles! Hearing a train was to be unloaded at Skorjist, I had Macgillycuddy saddled and rode off to Army headquarters 12 miles away. It was a frosty, starlit night. We cantered across frozen fields; snow crackled under his hoofs and he snorted with excitement. He loved adventure and, knowing something was afoot, the old boy went like mad. One *heard* the silence so tensely after days of shellfire. How black the sky was and how white the snow! And somewhere in that dark night the enemy were preparing; the enemy were ready and we were not! I thought of our men in the trenches with the thermometer many degrees below zero, facing a superior attacking force, without cartridges, and knew I had just got to find that ammunition train.

I arrived at Army headquarters and saw the Quartermaster General. I told him I must have all transport and he gave me full power to act. I gave the order to all the regiments of the Guard to send their horse transport to the Army headquarters at Myekov. Taking a motor I drove to the railhead at Keltsi about 70 miles away. Arriving, I went straight to the station-master, who I immediately perceived was a lazy fellow, more interested in the pretty nurses looking after wounded than in his very serious job. I asked him what had happened to the train bringing ammunition to the Guard Corps. He went into his fire-lit office to telegraph enquiries along the line. Some time later he reappeared with the news that he had got the answer that a train full of ammunition was about 20 miles away. I showed him the orders given me by Bezobrazov and told him to stop all transport on that line and bring the train immediately. Meanwhile lorries began to arrive at the station. It was about one at night. I waited till 3 A.M. The train did not arrive so I went to the Commandant of the station and asked him to explain the delay. He answered, "What can I do standing here? I can only telephone along the line."

I promptly warned him that if the train did not arrive he would be reported. This stimulated him to further telegraphing. Eventually he told me the train was on its way. I had all my transport men standing ready to unload. A shout of joy went up as the men dashed to the train. When the carriages were opened we found instead of shells only warm coats sent by mistake to us instead of to Siberia. Stiff with rage, I called the Commandant and told him that if he did not find the right train by dawn he would be shot on my responsibility. Taking out my revolver I sent him scuttling back to the telegraph office and all lines began to buzz as never before. Towards dawn the right ammunition train arrived. Like lightning the men who had waited all night threw themselves to work discharging the carriages, and one by one the lorries set off to Army headquarters, where horses were waiting to take their load to the anxious regiments. Each lorry made many journeys. During the hectic loading-up I dashed to and fro urging and instructing. One lorry caught fire and several stuck on the frozen road. Fire was not amusing with such cargo, and I summoned road workers to unload quickly and at the risk of their lives they got everything safely away. As we worked many wounded appeared walking laboriously along the road. All transport was otherwise engaged and they had to walk from the front, only to find no waiting-rooms or trains. In our desperate struggle we could not give any help to the poor fellows. One wretched man, shot through the body in three places, had walked 50 miles. Their despair at finding no warm waiting-room to lie down in until a train arrived made one's heart ache. The streets were full of wounded with no place to go and no-one to organize them. As I worked at the loading with sweat freezing to my face, I burnt inwardly with indignation and resolved to report the criminal negligence to General Bezobrazov the moment I got back. Only this capacity for suffering in silence has enabled the Russian masses to lie down under years of the Bolshevic régime.

The sun rose, gilding the untrodden snow around the labouring men. Unbelievably, the last lorry went off and I tore back to headquarters at Myekov. By noon, as the German shellfire began, the Guards had their ammunition and I was back with General Bezobrazov, a jibbering wreck, telling him of the ghastly plight of the wounded in Myekov and Keltsi.

A few weeks later the Emperor came to review the Guards. Unexpectedly he promoted me to the rank of Colonel and conferred on me a decoration. I thought, in fact, that he was singling me out to be reprimanded in front of all the Guards. There is no such rank in Russia as Major, but to go from Captain to full Colonel was a pretty good step up. Knox had teased me about being only a Captain when he was Lieut.-Colonel. I sent him a jubilant wire.

Fine sunny weather set in, with hard frosts at night. So many men were frozen to death that orders came through that the troops must keep their feet warm and be constantly supplied with hot tea. These instructions were greeted with grins. "Easy," laughed the men, "when all meals anyhow have to be carried to the trenches at the double under constant fire, and several men a day are killed or wounded in doing it."

Railways were blocked with warm clothing and munition trains had to wait. Every day Knox and I rode out over the crisp snow to various headquarters and villages. On December 1 I rode back from Myekov with the news of the battle of Lodz, in which the Germans lost 35,000 and the Russians 70,000. The Grand Duke was much upset that Joffre would not take the offensive in the West. We felt the whole burden of war lay on Russia's shoulders. At lunch that day General Bezobrazov waxed eloquent on the necessity of invading Silesia within a week, but Lodz had ended all hope of that for ever.

We changed headquarters to Yelcha, a few miles north. The Director of Equipment on the South-west Front arrived to take his son's body back to Petrograd. No wonder the service supply worked badly!

Thousands of new men poured to the front to fill our enor-

mous losses. Winter set in and with the terrible cold all fronts became stationary.

Christmas came and still the war went on. I went for a few
days to Warsaw, still the charming lighthearted city full of old
friends and packed with officers on leave, all desperately having a
good time. At the Bristol Hotel champagne was served in a teapot
and drunk with added relish from cups. I had never seen the city
so gay as that Christmas.

Strolling down the hotel corridor, I heard a well-known voice
and stopped dead. There was only one voice in the world like
that! "Feodor!" I shouted. Who should it be but Chaliapin, who
was giving concerts in the packed city. That night he came to my
room and sang for hours. The sweeping beauty he put into his art
affected one even more strongly after months of life at the front.
One had forgotten it existed—that enchantment. We talked till
dawn and, just talking with Chaliapin, one knew what great acting meant—for he permeated his conversation with funny peasant stories and his mimicry in relating them was unique. Such a
giant among men he was, not only in voice and figure but in soul.
When he came out onto the stage his personality overwhelmed
one, and that night, singing in the hotel bedroom, we trembled,
exulted and laughed with him. His voice swept the emotions of
an audience as a wave sweeps over the sand. He could express
everything: passion, loneliness, tenderness and cruelty, peasant
humour and Cossack war. All Russia was in his voice, all the
snow and beauty and madness that no other country knows.

Shortly before he died we met and recalled that night in the
ugly hotel bedroom with the brass bedstead and heavy red curtains. Talking and singing we had forgotten what was happening
in the world outside.

I don't think any troops celebrated Christmas as ours did. The
men in the trenches had trees decorated with silver paper and
sweets and packets of tobacco and presents from Petrograd. Poor
Knox on one of his serious military tours was invited to a party
and looked in vain for the children for whom he thought the
sparkling tree and bonbons were produced. The only children

present were bearded officers! Thirsting for information, he had to sit and sip tea while the staff strummed guitars! How we loved those feasts, that we felt might be our last. Russians could not help taking Christmas more seriously than war.

CHAPTER 14

The Impossible Struggle—January 1915

In 1914, the line of strategical deployment was advanced
solely in order to withdraw pressure from France . . .
Throughout the autumn and winter, in spite of the
severer climate, the war of movement and strenuous
fighting continued over a large part of the Eastern Theatre . . . Then shell and rifles began to fail and the Russians had to struggle alone through the bitter tragedy of
the retreat of 1915, their Western Allies being unready
as yet to render them effective assistance. —Winston
Churchill, *The Eastern Front*

IN JANUARY 1915 the Guard Corps were withdrawn to reserve
and then sent to Lomja, north of Warsaw. I motored with the
Staff of the Guard to Lomja. Knox rejoined us and we were allotted a good room together in the Imperial Bank. This room was
a nursery, which sounds charming, but the dear little children
had left their beds alive with bugs! Furiously I went to the Director of the Bank, who seemed quite unmoved on hearing the state
of his offspring. After much fuss Knox and I were transferred to
clean beds.

Walking out with Knox one afternoon we came on a long
line of carts filled with wounded, who were freezing to death
in the bitter cold while awaiting their turn to be carried into

hospital. Locals hung around gaping but did not offer to help. Knox and I suggested that they should fetch bread and hot tea for the wounded, and off they went, never having thought of it before. We soon got volunteers to help carry the wounded, and an old Polish woman took off her shawl and wrapped it around a wounded man, with tears running down her face. Girls appeared to help and bring cigarettes and apples. Inside the hospital organization seemed all right. The rooms were packed, but mattresses and blankets were clean and the building well heated.

Later that same day in the Staff I came on a young officer "examining" three prisoners. He could speak little German, and the tone of the whole affair was worthy of musical comedy, not of serious war. Bridge was being played in the next room and "Dummy" constantly strolled in to try his German on the prisoners, with the result that all questions got confused. I was furious. In my particular job I happened to see both sides of the question, that of the men who had fought so gallantly and were even now freezing, starving and dying in the trenches, and the hopelessly inadequate organization that let them give their lives needlessly. I was almost always in a state of inward indignation, which I vented chiefly on Knox, who reviewed events with the calm detachment of a British soldier.

"These people play at war," he said when I returned fuming with the tale of this interrogation.

"Ordre, contre ordre, desordre," muttered General B—— as in a single hour he received four contradictory orders from the Staff of the Army. The unfortunate 2nd Division of Guards and Guard Rifle Brigade which had marched 52 and 45 versts respectively the previous day were ordered to retrace their steps.

An attack was ordered on the morning of February 20. Knox and I rode out to see the centre of our front. A white mist prevented artillery fire till noon, then there was some muddle because a Cossack had *lost* a copy of Corps Orders *en route* to the Divisional Staff! The attack proving a failure, the 12th Army settled down for months of passive defence.

A few days later Knox and I rode to the headquarters of the

2nd Guard Division. We found the Staff gloomily eating lunch
in a hovel in a miserable village where it had retired the previous
day. While we were there the news came through that the Germans were preparing to attack. "I have an unpleasant bit of news.
Our battery wagons have been refused ammunition. We can fight
but not without shell."

The Divisional Commander said quietly, "You just tell the artillery to use shell as sparingly as possible." Thus war was waged.

On March 9 Bezobrazov told me the Guard had lost 10,173
officers and men in the last three weeks. Hindenburg wrote of
the terrible, incredible Winter Battle: "Have earthly beings really
done these things, or is it all but fable, phantom?" 100,000 Russians were killed in valiant, bitter fighting, 18 horses being needed
to pull one gun on roads of frozen mud.

On March 16 I accompanied General Bezobrazov to thank
the 2nd Division. Bezobrazov made a habit of personally visiting
units that had suffered severely. I followed in an open car. It was
bitterly cold. From the Divisional headquarters we rode (except
Knox, who could not stand the icy wind and preferred to walk).
Each unit was drawn up in line and the General, after greeting
and thanking the men for their gallant services, heartened them
with talk of future glories. It was touching to see how moved the
men were by his simple praise. Bezobrazov was very popular.

"Pauvres gens ils sont prets à donner leur vie pour une sourire,"
said Bezobrazov as we drove away. Knox was much struck by the
manner in which Bezobrazov, after a serious explanation of the
situation with officers in the trenches, would without any change
of voice add, "Remember also to pray. With prayer you can do
anything." The officers, crowded around with bearded faces, took
it all quite naturally, but the English regard God and emotion as
things to be rather embarrassed about—at least only to be mentioned in a "different tone of voice." Knox looked incredulous
and then shy when a discussion of military matters ended up with
a much-needed appeal to the Almighty.

The Declaration of War from the Winter Palace.
The crowd acclaims the Emperor, who can be seen on the balcony.

Morning start. Ilja, 1914.

Rodzianko with two orderlies. Lomja, 1915.

*The Grand Duke Nicolas,
Commander-in-Chief of the
Russian Forces, 1914–16.*

ABOVE: *General Sir Alfred Knox, Commander of the British Unit in Siberia, 1917–20.*

BELOW: *General Bezobrazov (second from left) inspecting the 2nd Division Front Lines at Lomja. Rodzianko to far right.*

Women digging trenches. Lomja.

Rodzianko as trooper in 10th Royal Hussars with two corporals. Tidworth, 1917.

Rodzianko as a private in the Royal Fusiliers. Hounslow, 1917.

Rodzianko as Staff Officer to General Knox.
Vladivostck, 1917–20.

CHAPTER 15

Tragedy—April, May, June 1915

The tale is one of hideous tragedy and measureless and largely unrecorded suffering. Considering the state of their armies and organization the Russian resistance and consistency are worthy of the highest respect. The strategy and conduct of the Grand Duke, bearing up amidst ceaseless misfortune, with crumbling fronts, with congested and threatened communications, with other anxieties still further in rear that most military commanders are spared, fills a chapter in military history from which a future generation of Russians will not withhold their gratitude. —Winston Churchill, *The Eastern Front*

UNARMED MEN had to be sent to the trenches to wait till their comrades were wounded or killed to take up their rifles. Every man knew this, knew the rifle handed to him came from a stricken soldier. Russian shell factories were unable to cope with the situation. The Grand Duke Serge, Inspector of Artillery, struggled with the need for increased production, but would not take the French hint to militarize labour in coal mines, as in France. Oh no! that would "resemble a return to serfdom"!

Knox, prowling about Petrograd, met an officer whose brother had gone to England to take over big guns.

"Does he know anything of gunnery?"

"No, he is a lawyer by education, an artist by inclination and a cavalry officer by occupation."

All this spring Kitchener urged Russia to place orders for ammunition abroad, but we argued that if Vickers failed nothing could be hoped from other foreign firms. The Grand Duke Serge had great ability, but it was said he loved the Artillery Department and its ways "as a man loves a woman though he knows she is a bad lot."

The production of shell in Russia increased enormously, but no one believed in the long war Kitchener foresaw.

In June gas was used by the Germans for the first time. The press announced our troops had had time to take "necessary measures." It later transpired these consisted of urinating on handkerchiefs and tying them around the face, for the respirators sent from Petrograd were lying undistributed in Warsaw. Over a thousand died from gas poisoning.

In June there were riots in Moscow as a result of discontent. My uncle, Michael Rodzianko, President of the Duma, maintained that the riots were the result of German intrigue which made use of popular dissatisfaction at Government inefficiency.

The peasants were getting good prices and had no cause for discontent, but in the towns food prices soared and Russia began to be definitely *bored* with the war. Men on leave spread stories of slaughter and suffering and people began to wonder what they were fighting for anyway. Was Serbia Russia's quarrel? Enthusiasm gradually died away and continual defeats made people wonder about the Government.

In April and May while spring stole over the war-stained country the Russian Army proved itself incapable in its weakened condition of standing up to any first-class Power.

My brother Serge had hurried through a military course at the Corps des Pages and was longing to get to the front. Just as he finished the course another four months was added to the officers' training. Desperately he appealed to me to "use influence." With the help of General Bezobrazov I got him into the Chevalier Guards with the rank of Sergeant. For some months we shared quarters at Lomja. Knox used the next room; his type-writer, clicking out reports, often went till four o'clock in the morning. I used to curse him for keeping me awake. One day he bought himself a fur hat of the Turkish fashion. In spite of my teasing, he fancied himself in it. One day we were walking in the village street when a sentry, thinking he looked very un-Russian, arrested him. Knox began to argue furiously in Russian, but his accent aroused more suspicion. Laughing heartily, I followed him to headquarters where he was of course released. Actually Knox's fine physique greatly impressed the Russian soldiers and peasants. "He's a fine fellow. He looks as if he could knock you down all right," they would whisper admiringly.

In April we began to retreat from Poland and the German advance started. Russian reinforcements poured in and the Army fought stubbornly but with little resistance, as local reinforcements caused muddle. All attacks were sheer murder owing to inadequate artillery preparation. As we were forced to save shell, the enemy could inflict loss unpunished.

Throughout June and July the Russian armies retired steadily. Russian losses up to July were three millions. Owing to lack of rifles, the calling up of the 1916 class was postponed.

When the Russian Command made a last effort to stem the German advance the Guard was transferred from the North-west Front and went southwards by train to Kholm in early July. Refugees were pouring eastwards to escape the German advance.

Our staff was lodged in a lovely Polish château at Reivets. Bezobrazov had been deprived of his best advisers. Beloved by his men, he had quarrelled with every Army Commander. For the first time in history the Prussian and Russian guards met. The Russians held their own, but late that night the whole line had to retire northwards.

Knox rode out with General Bezobrazov to thank the Izmailovski and Rifle Brigade for their courage in the fighting. They had lost 30 and 60 per cent respectively. That evening my General received orders from Lesh that he could attack as he had asked a few days previously. Bezobrazov thought the matter over and replied that the order was absurd. He issued undecided orders so that the Divisional Commanders telephoned asking if it was a "make-believe attack." As a result two corps advanced with heavy loss, and two other corps, awaiting the Guard attack, did not move.

General Bezobrazov was relieved of his command but told me he was sure to be reinstated. He drove off leaving General Olukhov in his place, and I remained as A.D.C. to the new Commander. A few days later, before General Olukhov had time to appreciate the incompetence of his Chief-of-Staff, the Germans started a bombardment. They attacked from the air and many bombs fell in Reivets village. As I rode through the little street a woman came up to me asking questions. She seemed quite normal and was unaware that a piece of her skull had been blown away and I could see her brains. I sent her to the hospital and a doctor told me that although chattering away she could not live.

Then orders suddenly came from the Army Staff to retire northwards. At 3 A.M. I charged furiously to the top of the château, where Knox and the other officers slept, to tell them to get ready to move. Cross, sleepy faces looked at me. An old Baltic Colonel called loudly for his sword, saying the Guard could die but not retreat (at any rate not at this hour). Fuming with rage, most of the Staff drove off to Army headquarters. Our Polish host remained in his precious château but nearly all the peasants left along with our troops. They were frightened to be left without protection, and carrying pathetic little bundles of rubbish, all their worldly belongings, they followed the marching soldiers. Dawn came greyly, lighting scenes of misery. We stopped for breakfast at a cottage where women made us tea while weeping with terror at the approaching Germans.

Several nights later we retired blowing up railroads and burning crops as we went. At each halting-place we had to destroy large quantities of the alcohol distilled on Polish estates, as this was too much temptation for the retreating troops. At Khilin the spirit was run along a channel to a marsh while soldiers lounged about with a thirsty gleam in their eyes. Finally the Commandant set fire to the spirit. The whole river glowed. Knox's orderly, a fine Cuirrassier of the Guard, and some others, found a hole in the distillery wall and they had a good swig of raw spirit. At midnight, time to move on, he was discovered dead drunk in the stable. Next day he apologized that he had been affected by "strong tea." Knox did not have him punished and we watched with secret amusement, for all that day he moved slowly and gently and the throb of his head jogging along those rough roads must have given him food for thought. He never did it again.

Throughout that summer Russians faced ceaseless German attack. We were weakened and in the worst stage of munitions supply. Wisely the Grand Duke ordered the retreat in good time on a front of 800 miles.

We heard that Warsaw had been abandoned, but the Russian men were quite happy to "retreat to the Urals, by which time the enemy will have dwindled to a single German whom we will kill and a single Austrian who will surrender." We were all thinking of 1812, never dreaming of an internal crash.

Knox wrote: "The regular officers of the Russian Army, who worked with their units throughout this great retreat and fought their way back yard by yard without losing heart or allowing their men to despair, were citizens of whom any country should be proud." How poorly have their services been rewarded! Officers used to beg to be allowed to fire "just one or two shots" and had to be refused.

In August, after Warsaw, the fortresses of Novogeorgievsk, Kovno, Grodno and Brest-Litovsk fell in steady succession. The whole of the Polish peasantry seemed to be moving eastwards. They could not stay for fear of the Germans, and thousands of refugees with carts and little flocks followed the retiring Russian troops. They did not know where they were going; neither did we. In frightful misery they died of starvation and sickness by the wayside. How many children were buried by worn-out mothers on that tragic exodus? How many were simply lost and never found again by their parents? The refugees used to dig themselves underground caves and live in the cold damp earth. Of course epidemics broke out.

In one burnt-out village we found a little pig all alone amongst the deserted ruins. He was so *in-apropos* somehow, that fat, pink squeaking creature. I adopted him and he became a delicious pet. I taught him to jump and his muscles developed beautifully. Alas, one day I had to leave him with our Red Cross unit. A week later I returned to find they had run short of rations and my orderly sorrowfully broke the news that he had been eaten.

CHAPTER 16

Summer & Autumn 1915—
Spring & Summer 1916

The Russian Command spends its time teaching the
Russian soldiers to die instead of teaching them how to
conquer. —Major-General Knox, 1915

In spite of internal catastrophes and military failures war
dragged on. After the fall of Warsaw I was sent to Petrograd to
see about supplies. Defeats at the front had caused the opposition
to grow. Now was the moment to get concessions and promises
and intrigues began in the Duma and in all organizations.

In September 1915 our Chief-in-Command, the Grand Duke
Nicolas, was dismissed, and against the advice of his ministers
the Tzar took personal command of the Armies. At the wish of
the Tzarina the Grand Duke, whom Hindenberg praised as the
best military brain in Europe, was relegated to the Caucasus. We
all knew she governed the interior and, influenced by Rasputin,
appointed all kinds of men to ministerial posts. Backed by his
beloved wife, the Tzar was convinced that all he did was right.
The Tzarina is often blamed for the fall of Russia, but the captain
of a ship is responsible, not his wife.

The Grand Duke's dismissal caused a sigh to go up from
the whole Army. He was known as a brilliant and honest man

who stood above court intrigues. On one occasion Rasputin telegraphed him asking permission to go to the front and bless the troops. The Grand Duke telegraphed back two pithy Russian words which can be clumsily translated as "Yes, do come. I'll hang you." The great soldier's departure caused consternation and depression.

The great tragedy of the Russian front lay in the corruption of officials and mismanagement of railways, which destroyed the heroic efforts of soldiers and officers who flung their lives recklessly away for the Russia they believed in. In September Knox wrote, "If ever a Government richly deserved a revolution it is the present one in Russia."

Steadily the Russians withdrew but Hindenberg's bold plans failed owing to the smallness of his forces and the calm nerve of our General Staff. In spite of the ground lost our armies were saved.

I travelled from Molodechno to Minsk and was approached at every station by deputations of peasants complaining that bands of Russian deserters were hiding in the woods and living by robbery.

In Minsk the Government allowed the Jews to close their shops on three successive days, with the result that hungry deserters broke into the shops and took what they wanted without paying. I went to the Chief-in-Command, General Ewath, and told him frankly there was danger of revolution. He answered: "Don't worry, there will be no revolution. It is your uncle in the Duma who arranges revolutions." However, he placed troops at the disposal of the town Commandant to maintain order.

Thousands of men reported sick and used any excuse to get away from the front. "What is the good of us fighting? We always get beaten!" Their logic was unfortunately understandable.

About this time Russia began to feel badly about the Western powers, who were always wanting her to attack to save themselves. Feeling became very bitter, and perhaps England and France did not realize that Russia, in spite of her huge size, was doing her utmost, more for their sakes than for her own. If Germany had won the war it would have mattered terribly to France, very little to Russia.

In September I was sent to Petrograd to see about supplies. Everyone was working hard there. At the beginning of the war Father had distinguished himself by sending a trainload of sweets to the nurses but now he was commanding reserves and he could always do a soldier's job well. Returning to the Staff of the Guards, I met Knox at Dvinsk. I had intended to go straight to Vilna, but Knox said things were serious and advised me to make a detour via Molodechno, 50 miles east of Vilna. Unknown to anyone the German Cavalry had advanced, severing the line between Dvinsk and Vilna, and were making a raiding expedition following my tracks. I had to do the 50 miles from Molodechno to Vilna by car along a hot and sandy road. At a small village about half-way the radiator began to boil. I stopped at a well to refill. Suddenly I noticed shooting and soldiers moving among the houses I had just passed. The men approached shouting furiously, and to my consternation I saw they were German Cavalry preparing to chase me. I jumped into the car and set off along the road at full speed. Bullets whizzed around but happily none hit the tyres. By the time I reached Vilna the news of the German Cavalry march had reached headquarters and I was greeted with amazement. I was the last person to get through the line.

As we were surrounded the order came to retreat to Dvinsk. One night during the retreat I slept in a half-destroyed cottage. As I dozed off something crept up my body and over my face. I was too tired to push it away till I felt a long tail and knew it for a rat. Then I shouted!

The troops fought their way back for three days, losing many men. Eventually we entrenched near Dvinsk where the line remained more or less unbroken for two years. The Guard had to be thoroughly reorganized for the best men had gone. We went into reserve and for the seventeenth time the ranks were filled with reinforcements. As the second winter set in, cold again caused a pause at all fronts.

In 1916 the munitions crisis began to pass but Germany regarded Russia as beaten. By early spring the Guards were reorganized, their dilapidated ranks filled with fine new men. The Command of the Guards was returned to Bezobrazov and a new Guard Army formed. When we were finally ready, commencement of operations was delayed as the Tzar wished to review the Guards before handing it over to the Commander-in-Chief of the South-west Front. A short offensive ended speedily when, owing to lack of foresight, the 7th Army was reduced to starvation.

Russia had scarcely any aeroplanes and the German flyers wrought havoc over our lines. Finding success easy, their pilots became more and more daring. They would fly over the lines, land in a covered place and let out spies in Russian uniform. The front was too vast to be properly controlled.

An extraordinary instance occurred near Rogishche. A German landed in a field surrounded by woods. Finding he had made a mistake he was about to set off again, when a cow that had been peacefully grazing, suddenly charged his machine. She killed herself but so damaged the propeller that the aeroplane would not rise, and hearing the roar of engines some Guards captured the German. He was brought in swearing volubly while our men made a legend of the "patriotic cow."

My uncle, President of the Duma, was optimistic in spite of the muddled internal situation. In towns the burden of war was greatly felt, in spite of abundance of necessities in the country. Distribution was so badly organized that food queues at food shops and for trams in the cold were long though needless. Officers' wives in Petrograd lived on the flour and sugar their husbands sent them from the front. The people suffered but remained docile. Uncle said: "Some people may favour peace but they dare not speak. Rasputin will not work for peace for he is run by a ring of banks who make money out of the war. Russia is all right if only England would help her more with guns and money."

No-one dared speak to the Tzar about Rasputin. No-one even dared arrest the monk when he smashed up night clubs. Russia had abundance of men but too few officers. About this time I first began to hear talk of a revolution. A clever officer said there would certainly be a revolution, the army having completely changed owing to the death of so many of the well-trained pre-war officers. A great mistake was the way in which men were sent to any regiment instead of serving in one particular regiment and believing it the best in the Army.

A concentration started towards the north. Two Guard Corps set off to help the 2nd Army. In spite of new munitions the Russian attack at Noroch failed. The day before the attack thaw set in and the front became a lake. 70,000 were killed.

Spring came. No Russian will work underground in the summer and there was no question of compulsion. Shortage of steel arose from lack of labour in the coal mines. France did not permit strikes during the war, but Russian workmen took a day off whenever they felt like it. Disgusted, the French sent the Socialist M. Albert Thomas to inspect and advise. His autocratic ways amazed Russia, but compulsory labour sounded too much like "a return to serfdom." Russia would lose the war rather than do anything to upset an idea.

Drearily we realized the struggle had been going on for two years with tremendous and unnecessary losses. Much was expected from Lord Kitchener's visit. We thought his advice and influence would bring about important changes. His immense prestige would induce the Tzar to listen to him if to no-one else. We could not believe it when the Hampshire went down and we heard that Kitchener had been drowned. The whole Army groaned. Their last hope of influencing the Emperor had vanished.

General Wolfe Murray arrived instead. I was attached to him and accompanied him on big inspections of the Russian Armies. We had many discussions and I tried to make him see the discontent of the fighting men was due to lack of organization and ammunition, with terrific uncontrolled revolutionary propaganda going on.

"You exaggerate," he said. "Look at your brilliant reserves."

"It's all very well to see them as in reserve, but these men are not trained properly. The best are gone. When they get into the firing line they change."

The troops *had* fought brilliantly. I saw them, brave men dying like tigers, but terrible, unnecessary losses broke their spirit. Russia ordered her best men to the front lines and wasted them. They were mown down without being able to fire a shot simply because their ammunition did not arrive in time. In vain I argued: General Wolfe Murray was deceived by the fine physique of the Guards. He had not seen men attacking machine-guns with revolvers in their hands.

The Russian Command prepared for an advance around Krevo. Under Bezobrazov the new Guard Army entrained northwards. Careful preparations were made for the attack and in July the Guards were thrown forward between the 3rd and 8th Armies in a last desperate bid for Kovel.

This surprise attack, known as Brusilov's Offensive, proved the greatest Russian victory. It was a complete success, but it was important to hold what had been gained and not return to trench warfare so unsuited to Russian temperament. In spite of harrowing and unnecessary losses and the fact that all successes were handicapped by the weakness of railways, which prevented following up; in spite of deserters and costly, barren attacks, the rare gallantry of Russian soldiers continued. They fought for Russia, and that was all they knew.

CHAPTER 17

Operations of Guard Army on Stokhod—
The First Mutterings of Revolution—
July 21 to August 12, 1916

Aᴄᴛᴇʀ ᴛʜᴇ ʀᴇᴛʀᴇᴀᴛ from Vilna the Guard Army was carefully nursed. We went to Bessarabia, to Volhynia, then north to Dvina, and to Molodechno for the Kovno offensive. The Guards travelled much without being under fire, being retained for a great occasion, which the forcing of the River Stokhod seemed to be.

It was July 1916 and the great Eastern Offensive was now ordered. The Guards under General Bezobrazov advanced to the first line, taking up a section of the front between the 3rd and 8th Armies. The idea was to break through at one spot and let the Cavalry charge the Germans . . . a ridiculous plan. During two days' constant fighting the two Guard Corps made good all ground on the right bank. As usual, artillery preparation was insufficient, but the Rifle Division was ordered to charge after forty-eight hours' feeble bombardment of the enemy lines. By a criminal mistake the section chosen for the attack was a bog. As they went forward, wading through marsh up to their middles, the men sank and were drowned. The Germans on higher ground kept up machine-gun fire and simply mowed down the struggling men. On they came; climbing over the sinking bodies of their comrades, wave after wave of grey figures clambered on. After terrific efforts they captured a low hill, but at a loss of 70 per cent of their numbers. The terrible courage of those men who waded on and on is unrecorded in the histories of the war: the country they died for was soon to crash; their sacrifice was in vain.

During this attack the Guards lost 53,000 officers and men, and that loss was unnecessary. We had gained a few versts but abandoned a good position for one less easy to defend.

The Grand Duke Paul, Commander of the 2nd Corps, now blamed Bezobrazov for "wasting the Guard," but General Brusilov, Commander of the South-west Front, had laid down the exact position the Guard Corps were to take up on the German front. A disagreement resulted. The Grand Duke Dimitri (son of the Grand Duke Paul) set off to see the Emperor at headquarters, and defend his father and General Brusilov. On the same day I was dispatched by General Bezobrazov with a personal letter of explanation to His Majesty. I drove to Rovno and caught the Grand Duke's train. He gave me a seat in his wagon, but warned me I would have to find my own way from Mogilev, as he was determined to get his say in first. He was going to defend his father, I to defend my General. We had an interesting, friendly journey, though each knew exactly what the other was up to. On arriving at Mogilev I was scheming how to get to the Emperor first. We learnt the Empress had just arrived on a visit and the Grand Duke naturally thought he would find him in her carriage. I tore off to headquarters, where I found General Alexeiev, and by good luck the Emperor was with him. He gave my letter straight to His Majesty. Next day at lunch the Tzar, worried and horrified by my account of the battle, said to me: "Tell General Bezobrazov I am more than satisfied with the action of the men, but he is to be careful of the lives of my beloved Guardsmen."

In triumph I returned to Bezobrazov at Rodishche with the dispatch, and the Tzar's thanks were read out in the orders of the day in all the Guard regiments. I thought all was well, but five days later Bezobrazov's orderly suddenly came to tell me to prepare to leave at once with my General. We packed and went to headquarters at Mogilev. Bezobrazov saw the Tzar, who kissed him and told him to take six weeks' leave before returning to his command. Bezobrazov went off to Petrograd hoping against hope he would soon be called back, but his military career was finished. Nevertheless, sure that he would get the Guard back, Bezobrazov asked the Emperor's permission to keep me as A.D.C. in Petrograd. Feeling was bitter there at the Guards' failure.

Lady Muriel Paget, who had done such great work with the Anglo-Russian Red Cross, was then in Petrograd, and I had the honour to present her with the decorations given her by the Emperor. Her four medals of St. George were well earned indeed.

My youngest brother, Victor, had finished the Corps des Pages and was now a full-blown officer in the Guards Artillery. He became engaged to General Bezobrazov's daughter, who was a trained nurse. Serge wrote that he had been made a Lieutenant and won a St. George's Cross. It was incredible how two years of war had made the two boys grow up. I still thought of them in socks and sailor suits as Mother had always insisted on dressing them, even when they were much too big, regarding them as her babies!

Petrograd was hot in August, and, after two years' almost constant work, I applied for leave and went off for three weeks in the country. I took Macgillycuddy to the "Wolf's Den" and left him there with my other horses. Then I joined my children, who were back at Usviat in White Russia. Will I ever forget that last visit, riding up through the honey-scented woods to the white château perched on a hill among miles of virgin forest? How peaceful it was, like riding into Fairyland, with the wonderful smell of flowers that only our Russian earth can give, and the still, green lakes so quiet and undisturbed.

My children were full of the German scare when they had been hurried off to Petrograd. Every day we rode through the endless moss-carpeted forests and swam in the lakes, to the consternation of wild duck, who had never before seen such strange white otters. What laughter was caused when I threw my son into deep water to make him swim and, slipping, fell in myself, in uniform!

Writing this in the civilized serenity of modern England, I can hardly believe that from my bedroom window one could sometimes see bears going down to the lakeside to drink. Their pug marks and those of wolves would be found in the morning.

When a Russian peasant dies they hold a vigil as in Ireland. The body is washed, dressed and laid out. The priest watches all night and for three days the women wail, and neighbours come to mourn and incidentally eat a good many funeral cakes. Of course my little son was determined to go and see his "first corpse." Having a morbid childish imagination, when night fell he could not get the white face out of his mind, but was ashamed to admit his terror after a day of boasting.

Late that night I heard voices in the orchard, where the night watchman had a busy time preventing boys stealing apples. There was Pavlic, white and shaking, talking to the watchman, who hardly calmed his nerves by telling hair-raising stories of corpses who had "woken up," etc. Our English governess could no longer control the boy and I thought it time to get a tutor, but in Russia every man had been called up.

Still from the near-by villages bands of peasants were marching off to join the Army. In the dusk one saw them go, always singing. To the very end they sang.

The weeks passed like a dream. The last day we drove over to our adjoining estate, Pudst, an older castle that in former days, took a long day's journey on horseback. Ney had passed through Usviat with his army and both places bore scars of the Napoleonic wars.

My leave ended, I went off. Looking back I can see Usviat as it was that last time, pale as an ivory castle against the blue evening clouds. Unreal, enchanted land of abundance, I did not know that I left for ever.

At the end of September General Bezobrazov went to the Caucasus to see the Grand Duke Nicolas and I accompanied him as A.D.C. The journey was most interesting. We saw all the new formations being sent out to this front; they seemed in good condition and well equipped. We spent several days in Tiflis, and I

saw my brother-in-law, Prince Sasha Chavchavadze, who commanded a Circassian Horse Regiment. It took a good officer to
command the respect of these fighters, and Sasha, a real Georgian, understood them and was adored.

When we returned to Petrograd I realized that General Bezobrazov was not going to return to the front and decided to go to
headquarters at Mogilev for instructions.

The night before leaving I dined with the British Ambassador, Sir George Buchanan, a true friend of Russia who realized
the seriousness of the situation and had in vain done his best to
explain things to the Tzar.

After dinner he asked everyone to stand up, and unexpectedly
presented me with a C.M.G. in the name of the King of England.

I was entirely taken aback by this honour. In the pause that
followed, Lady Georgina Buchanan, who, with her daughter had
done great work for the soldiers and in the Anglo-Russian Hospital, came up and we began to chat about Knox. And then she told
me, hesitatingly, with the real modesty of one who had achieved
great things, of the difficulties arising from the fateful and critical nature of affairs around them. She had the keenest apprecia-
tion of the way in which these difficult times were lightened, as
all grim things invariably are, by the unconscious humour that
must always arise when two races meet. I felt once more the fundamental characteristics of sympathy and understanding which
attract Englishmen and Russians together, no matter what tem-
porary accidents may separate them.

On arriving at Mogilev I had a long conversation with General
Voyeikoff; he scoffed at my descriptions of revolutionary propaganda. "You exaggerate," he said. The words General Wolfe Murray had used.

The Emperor, who since assuming Supreme Command had
spent most of his time at headquarters, invited me to lunch. After
the meal he called me into his room for a private talk. He told me
he had received urgent telegrams from the King of Italy and from
France and England calling for a Russian offensive to ease pressure on the Western fronts.

"You know yourself," he said, "the Guards are in reserve and we cannot advance this winter. By spring we will be ready. You have seen a lot of our front and I would like you to go to Italy and explain the situation."

I asked how long I would remain in Italy.

"At least five months."

I went back to Petrograd to fix up papers and get a diplomatic passport. Then I went to the front and visited my brother in the trenches and also the Guard Rifle Brigade Ambulance, who since the beginning of the war had done wonderful work. The strain of looking after suffering men was often worse than real fighting.

On one occasion the Ambulance Unit had been lost during a retreat for two days. Then Bezobrazov sent me out to search. It was a dark night and hard to find anything. I rode Macgillycuddy through woods and deserted villages. At last I found them; doctors and nurses were lying in a hut exhausted, sleeping on the floor too worn out to move, or even carry away the dead bodies lying beside them. Somehow I forced them up and got them back to Brest-Litovsk. The constant responsibility was enough to wear away anyone's nerves and some of them were verging on a breakdown.

When my papers were ready I reported to the Emperor at headquarters for final instructions. During a long conversation I asked him for permission to take my children with me and leave them in England *en route*.

"But you are only going for six months!"

"Sir, it is impossible to get tuition for my son in Russia. As you know, every man is called to arms and one cannot tell how long the war will go on." I could not explain my secret feeling of dread that made me want to get them out of Russia.

"Do as you wish," he said.

Then suddenly as I went out of the door he called me back. "Aren't you afraid of risking your family with submarines? Well, be careful, and good luck. On your return I'll see that you get a regiment to command."

I thanked him, but somehow this kind promise did not fill

me with excitement as it should have. I am the most unpsychic of people, but when the Emperor said good-bye to me I felt that it was the last time. Something extraordinary in his eyes made me know we would never meet again. What is it, that curious inner awareness that the soul has of death? I will never forget that strange last look.

In Petrograd disturbances had already begun. A discontented, sinister atmosphere had grown up and officers as well as troops openly criticized the Royal Family in a way that would have been impossible a few months earlier. Everywhere one heard: "What to expect? The Empress is a German." In vain the Commanders-in-Chief warned the Tzar that soldiers' letters showed that they wrote constantly of the Empress and Rasputin; in vain they implored him to change his policy.

I visited Knox, who was in bed with scarlet fever, and he seemed pessimistic enough. At the end of December, a few days before we were to sail, Mother called me from my packing.

"Paul, what do you think? Rasputin has been killed. Apparently Felix Yousoupoff and the Grand Duke Dimitri are involved and there is tremendous excitement at the Palace . . ."

"Thank God, but it's a bit late."

"Poor Empress. You can imagine the state she is in over her little son . . ."

"What *will* happen now, I wonder?"

The extraordinary thing was that when Rasputin was present the Tzarevitch never was ill, the moment the monk left he got an attack. Whether this was due to drugs or hypnotic influence one cannot say, but there lay the scoundrel's hold over the Empress.

Next morning my servant brought me the paper and I saw he was longing to talk about something.

"What do you think about it?" he asked, bristling with excitement. I saw a small paragraph mentioning Rasputin's death.

"What do YOU think, Ivan?"

Shaking his head, he refused to answer. That day the whole city knew that Yousoupoff and the Grand Duke were arrested. No one talked of anything else and most people expressed great relief, but, alas, the murder came too late. That queer unsavoury scandal had sullied the Imperial house throughout Russia.

Just before I left, the Chevalier Guards were ordered to Petrograd from the front to maintain order in case of trouble. It is interesting to recall that officers of my regiment were seriously discussing the advisability of forcing the Tzar to grant a Constitution. The Iron Autocrat had gone and even his most loyal regiment felt that he had betrayed himself. Yet as the German, Maximilian Harden, so truly wrote: "Nicolas Alexandrovich whom only light minds can already name the last of the Tzars, sought to establish peace firm as a rock, summoned the nations to disarm and banished alcohol from Russia. That he willed these three things History will some day write down to his credit. His conquerors, who gave themselves out to be Saviours of Mankind, universal Messiahs, have worked more horror and woe in eight months than he wrought in eight years."

CHAPTER 18

January 1917—London—Italy—
The March Revolution—I Join
the British Army

> Historians of the war should have nothing but admira-
> tion for the chivalrous strategy of the Russian Supreme
> Command. The Grand Duke Nicolas and later the Em-
> peror had a single guiding idea . . . to do their utmost
> with the means at their disposal to lighten the burden
> of the Allies. —Knox

ONE GREY DAY in January we left Petrograd, little dreaming, in
spite of rumours brewing, that it was for the last time. Via Finland, Sweden and Norway we reached Bergen and there boarded
the English boat *Jupiter*. This ship was supposed to be safe from
submarines because spies of both sides were reputed to cross on it!
I don't think even the children enjoyed the trip much, it was so
cold and rough. Lifebelts were always on, and the wild, dark skies
had a depressing effect.

In England I found a girls' school for Tamara and settled Paul
at Harrow. After a few rushed days in the strangely transformed
war-time London, I travelled on to Italy and reported to Prince
Volkonski, the Military Attaché in Rome. From there I went to
Italian headquarters at Udine to report to Colonel Enkell, Senior
Officer of the Russian Mission.

"It will be difficult for you to see the King," he said; "while in the trenches he receives no one."

Colonel Enkell sent me to see General Cadorna, Commander-in-Chief of the Italian Army. We had an interesting discussion and he advised me to return to Rome for a few days. He would wire me when I could see the King.

At the Embassy in Rome there was plenty to do and for several weeks I was kept extremely busy getting munitions sent off to Russia. Volkonski sent me on trips all over the place and I went several times to Paris. I was at the Crillon on Good Friday when one of Big Bertha's shells, fired eighty miles away, exploded, several people being killed.

At last we knew that Russia, with munitions pouring in, was actually ready for a great attack.

General Cadorna sent a message that I could return to the Italian front, as I might be granted an interview with the King; but soon bad news began to leak through from Russia. The Allies, startled by Germany's recovery, were planning a huge united attack on all fronts simultaneously, and knowing that my country was at long last sufficiently equipped they expected victory. Germany decided that only revolution could bring peace with Russia. The Bolshevics offered possibilities that could never be won from the Tzar. The feeling of revolution impending which had been in the air when I left Petrograd was augmented by the tactics and aggressive behaviour of the Government towards the Duma and the People's Party headed by my uncle.

In the Embassy we continued work and got large consignments of ammunition sent off, but the situation was most worrying. Regular fighting began in Petrograd, and the exasperated country turned its wrath on the Tzar. In vain the Duma appealed to the Emperor. My uncle said the Tzar could not understand that the Duma was not opposing him, but standing between him and revolution. At the end of February the Duma, refusing to be dissolved, formed a committee to be joined to the Government. Headed by my uncle, members of the Duma made the round of the regiments, delivering brilliant speeches and urging the soldiers to continue the fight with Germany. Unfortunately this was just what they did not feel like doing.

In numberless telegrams my uncle implored the Tzar (who was all the time at headquarters) to make concessions, but he was not heeded—and what good indeed could a Constitution have done at that wild, disastrous moment? The Duma was forced to take revolutionary measures. Still making efforts, my uncle telegraphed the Tzar at headquarters: "Position serious . . . Anarchy in capital . . . Essential to entrust some person who possesses the country's confidence with formation of new government . . . Procrastination fatal."

At the Embassy we were kept glued to the telegraph wires but none of us dreamed of the crash to follow. I no longer tried to get in touch with the King of Italy, for what sense would my message have now? The Tzar was no longer on the throne.

The news that reached the Embassy was chaotic but one never thinks anything too unpleasant will last. My mother wrote me from Petrograd, "We are awaiting events," and unfortunately that was what most Russians did, till the events came and swirled them out of existence. Yet the Revolution and all that was to follow was not unforeseen. There were great brains in Russia who predicted clearly and in detail exactly what would befall their country. But of these men of intellect and vision, meditating, reading and philosophizing in their remote castles, not one stood up to stem the tide. The field was left to men of action with slogans and no pity; the most unscrupulous won. Of the intelligentsia and aristocracy, though many had vision, none took up Russia's cudgel; impassive and mystic they stood by, while Revolution swept their world away.

A delegation of mutineers visited the Duma, now installed in the Tauride Palace, to ascertain their attitude. My uncle defined the task of the moment as the replacement of the old régime by a new form of government, and asked for order and calmness. He formed a committee for the "Preservation of Order," which included representatives of all parties, including the Socialist Kerenski.

At first, like many others, I hoped the Revolution would clear out what was rotten in the Russian system. We did not expect the old régime to turn straight into anarchy. The country outside Petrograd remained unarmed and inarticulate. The fantastic, child-like credulity of the simple peasant soldiers made the Army easy to break up. Most of the trained soldiers had been killed and others were sick of it. "Strict" officers were dismissed, while babyish reasoning held some regiments together. The soldiers were quite happy to live quietly in the trenches and be well fed by the Government as long as they were not asked to attack. They received propaganda with cattle-like docility and were always impressed by the latest agitator.

By April the efficiency of the Army was ruined and officers began to shoot themselves. All who tried to instil order were driven from their regiments. In desperation a regiment of Russian women was formed. They marched long distances and accomplished quite a lot, but that sort of army does not last long! I do not think they awed the Germans, but a Prussian officer they captured committed suicide from mortification.

Realizing the hopelessness of the situation, I determined to leave Rome and return to London, join the British Army and carry on. The Embassy was no longer in touch with Petrograd and our agent wrote that he could send no more money. I sold my car and horses and just managed to pay the hotel bill. The manager was charming. It was the same hotel in which I had given the famous party.

I was in Rome when the battle of Caporetto took place. Everyone knows the story of that disaster. Actually the Italian Cavalry behaved with great heroism that day, but the world prefers to scoff rather than to admire those who were killed trying to stem the tide.

On reaching London I found it was not so easy for a "foreign" Colonel with a diplomatic passport to become a British Tommy. I tried to join at Scotland Yard, but they asked to see my papers, and seemed doubtful of accepting me. Discouraged, I walked home. On the way I met an old friend, Colonel Thornhill, whom I had known in Petrograd when, with Knox, he was attached to the Embassy. He had just come on leave from Petrograd and told me of the situation there, where lorries of wounded Cossacks were stopped and the dying men beaten to death. But Kerenski's flabby Provisional Government had not yet given way to the Committee of the Soviet, and worse horrors were to follow.

As we walked along Whitehall I asked Thornhill to fix me up. He had to leave for Petrograd next day but kindly took me straight to Colonel Steel in the War Office and explained my situation. I got permission to enlist in the Royal Fusiliers. Next day I reported at Hounslow Barracks. The feeling of being a soldier again lightened my heart and some of my terrific depression faded. Having passed the medical exam., I was dressed in a private's uniform. The Adjutant asked if I was married and had children, and their addresses.

"Yes, sir. My daughter at boarding school and my son at Harrow."

He looked puzzled and rather distrustful. A queer foreign element was not to his likes in the army! Next day I was surprised and amused to find myself attached to a battalion composed of Poles, Russians and Jews from East London. A curious mixture of foreigner and Cockney, they jabbered away in their various accents and dialects, and I felt about as conspicuous as a large polar bear in a company of lively dogs. Most of them came to my shoulder.

A few weeks later Colonel Steel sent for me at the War Office. "Rodzianko, I want you to help me collect stranded Russian officers for the British Army. They will be useful."

This work could not have been more to my taste. I knew of many poor fellows suddenly left without a country, feeling it was hopeless to go back to that mad mess, who were delighted to get the chance of fighting for their Russia though in a foreign uniform.

One afternoon in January 1918, while returning down Sloane Street, who should I meet but General Knox, whom I had not seen since visiting him in Petrograd a year ago. I saluted my old friend respectfully. He stared at me in amazement while recognition slowly dawned in his face.

"How the devil did you get into this uniform?" he asked.

"Sir, I am now a private in His Majesty's Army," I replied, and told him the tale of the last few months. Laughing, he asked me to his house, where we had a long talk. I don't know who had most to say. He told me of the last year in Russia, of how Kerenski had kicked out my uncle, of the weak Provisional Government, of Kerenski's fall and the failure of brave Kornilov. In October he had dined with my mother to meet my brother-in-law, Prince Sasha Chavchavadze, who commanded the Circassian Horse Regiment which marched on Petrograd at the head of Krasnov's forces. Sasha gave an amusing account of how they came on the Pavlovski Regiment drawn up to "defend the Revolution" and the whole battalion fled. The lion-hearted Caucasians thought they had stumbled on manœuvres and in the end the whole Pavlovski Regiment joined them and walked gaily to Army headquarters.

Chavchavadze's proud mountaineers were forbidden by their religion to touch alcohol and they had been pretty disgusted at Kalusz, where 4000 drunken soldiers violated old women and children of eight in the streets. Forty or fifty took each woman and cut off their arms and breasts when they had finished. The soldiers lay drinking wine out of gutters while the brave Caucasians watched coldly these "Christian" savages who had conquered their fathers.

My mother, he said, had been in her usual energetic frame of mind, denouncing "these men who change their governments as often as they change their loves." Undaunted by the chaotic state of the country, she continued to believe in Russia's power to pull together, and when Knox suggested taking her jewels over to England for safe keeping she ticked him off: "How can you suggest anything so unpatriotic? My jewels are in the bank and belong to Russia."

Her little grandson, Paul Chavchavadze, stayed with her at

this time, and tells a charming tale of how, after the first Revolution, Mama was advised to cut down household expenses. Did she sack any of the white-coated chefs eating their heads off in the kitchen? No. But she decided to cut down on the thing she detested most and had been ordered by the doctor. Sending for the head cook, she solemnly explained that he was to economize and *spinach* was not to appear again.

In his unboastful way Knox described how he had saved the courageous Woman's Battalion that was captured in the Winter Palace by the Bolshevic troops. To hear him tell it one would think it easy to drive to Bolshevic headquarters and literally force a procrastinating official to issue an order that the women be set free.

The 137 volunteers, after fighting desperately were badly beaten, were taken to the Grenaderski Barracks, to be outraged and probably tortured; but Knox, in spite of being a diplomat in a foreign country, felt that at least he would have no nonsense. Owing to him alone they were escorted to the Finland station and entrained for Levashova, to the rage of the brutes who were waiting to get them. A deputation of four women came to thank him and asked if they could not be transferred to the British Army as there was nothing more they could do to help Russia. Knox told them English women were not allowed to fight, and told the officers who accompanied them what he thought of them. "But these men were past all shame and the heroic effort of the women had no effect on them."

I could not believe his ghastly descriptions were of my country, my people. Russia seemed to have vanished. "The Bolshevic *coup d'état*," said Knox, "was the work of a handful of fanatics. It succeeded because they seduced by wine, money and promises the armed workmen and some of the garrison, and above all because Kerenski, in desiring to please the Moderate Socialists who were merely talkers, alienated the only men of action who might have helped him, the officers and Cossacks. Russia, the country, stood by passive."

"Peace at any price," was the way to consolidate their success. Knox had left Russia with Sir George Buchanan in January. Under Lenin, Trotski, Kamenev and Zinoviev, my country was to face its terrible destiny.

"Are you happy in your new regiment?" asked Knox, when I had told him the story of the last hectic months.

"It is wonderful to be in any army, but I wish I could get to the Cavalry."

A few days later the order suddenly came, I was to transfer to the 10th Hussars at Tidworth. Being supplied with a military ticket I blessed Knox and took the train, delighted at getting back to the atmosphere I loved. The 10th asked no questions and in a week's time I made friends with the men, who said they could not pronounce my "bloody name" but called me Paul. How good it was to get back to the clean smell of stables, to have horses to look after and simple, honest soldier's work to do. Carrying forage, grooming, and polishing, my frayed nerves recovered. For the first time for a year I began to be happy and tried never to think of what had happened to my own horses, who had been burnt along with Mishka and the other animals when the revolutionary madness reached the "Wolf's Den."

One day while walking in the yard the Sergeant-Major called me up and asked where we had met before. "Seems I know the look of you. Were you over with the Russian team at Olympia four years ago?"

I asked him not to reveal who I was, but somehow it must have leaked out among the men, for every morning after this I found my boots and buttons cleaned when I woke. I could never find out who did, but nothing has ever touched me more than that simple, very English gesture.

Several weeks later the Colonel sent for me. "So you are Colonel Rodzianko who won the King's Cup?"

"Yes, sir."

"Well, you shall take my young officers under instruction."

I thanked him, but thought it would be rather awkward. He made me his orderly and I think I made a very good one, for I knew all the things not to do!

Every few weeks I was called up to London by Colonel Steel to report at the War Office on the subject of recruiting Russian officers. How strangely different London was; the streets were full of khaki, and cars loaded with bags of gas which replaced petrol. Bus conductors and ticket collectors were all women, and being a Tommy I found I had a great success with them and was always given first place.

Spring came, beautiful as ever in England, and I learned a lot from my comrades about "walking out." Their initiative often proved amazing. I could write a short but unprintable pamphlet on the technique of that time-honoured sport as devised and discussed in the British Army.

The funniest thing occurred when the W.A.A.C.s were placed in the middle of the camp. I don't know what bright fellow thought that a lot of girls could be popped down in the midst of several thousand men about to go off to the front and probably be killed. Anyway he didn't know much. The women's buildings were surrounded by barbed wire and a sentry kept on duty at the entrance, but we were being taught to cut barbed wire, and the women, I must say, without meaning to be unchivalrous, were inclined to egg us on. The climax came when the men who had been practising charges all day decided to practise on the W.A.A.C.s at night. The sentry was overpowered and the building taken by force. What fun it was not to be an officer, to be able to join in, shout joyfully and not feel responsible! That night was worth a lot. The women were carried off shrieking and making a fuss but really enjoying it.

Of course the officers in charge rushed to restore order, but it took hours. No culprits could be traced and feminine giggles were heard all over the camp.

The idea of an Allied intervention to stop Bolshevism and pull Russia together was being discussed. I have clippings of several letters I was asked to write to *The Times* on the subject, urging that a strong, organized Russia was the only way to help England and France keep a strong hold on Germany now and always. Two examples are reprinted here.

TO SAVE RUSSIA FROM THE GERMANS

Plea for Armed Help

A private letter from a Russian officer in Paris describes the work of the Russian Legion, recently formed, and gives an interesting insight into the views of these Russian Allies in regard to the situation of their country and the necessity of Allied intervention.

The formation of the Legion is going on well, and one unit has already taken a successful part in the fighting against the Germans.

My chief care at present is to help my unfortunate country to become once more a Great Power, capable of fulfilling its duty as an Ally and of assuring safety of life and possessions to its subjects. I think that the only way in which Russia can be saved is by a friendly international intervention of all the Allies, based on armed force, around which it would be possible to begin the formation of a new Russian Army on proper lines.

All intelligent and sensible people in Russia are now waiting to be freed from the yoke of Bolshevism and to have some order and authority in the country. Unfortunately they see no possibility of introducing order so far, except by a German invasion. They must be convinced, not by words, but by deeds, that order can be re-established by their friends the Allies. Alexeieff, Korniloff, Kaledin, and others have been unable to achieve any decisive results because they had no foothold, which can be provided only by the intervention of the Allies.

Either Russia will right herself with the aid of the Allies and greatly strengthen their forces in the final and decisive stages of the war, or she will be organized by the Germans and become a hinterland enabling Germany to become invincible in the future. If we admit the latter possibility, it will mean that 200,000,000 of Slavs will reinforce the German world, and involve both Western Europe and the East, including India, in serious peril. Intervention is practicable at present as a means of helping Russia to combat Germany, but, once the war is over, it will become impossible.

The future of the British Empire, and particularly of India, depends upon our victory over Germany and upon the regeneration of Russia as a Great Power faithful to the Alliance. By saving Russia from chaos and from the Germans, France and England will not only hasten their own victory, but will assure their own future.

The fate of Europe hangs upon your decision, and there is no time to be lost.

ALLIED HELP FOR RUSSIA

To the Editor of the Times

Sir,—I have been asked many times to give my opinion on the much-discussed question of Allied intervention in Siberia. As a Russian and a Russian officer I consider it my duty to say what I think at this moment in the interest of my country and the Allies.

I have read reports to the effect that the movement of the Allied forces through Siberia to defend Russia against German aggression has been in principle decided. I sincerely hope this is true, for in my opinion such a course is the only one which will save the Allied cause in the East and Russia also. I strongly object, however, to the assumption that the Allies should acknowledge the Bolshevists before undertaking intervention. Do the people who talk so lightly of recognizing the Bolshevists know what Bolshevism means? All the Allies are fighting against the oppression of weak countries and condemn Germans for the way they have treated the civil populations of the captured territories. Are the Allies then going to support a Bolshevist Government which is terrorizing, robbing, pillaging, and murdering its own people? Do they know that more than 8000 Russian officers have been murdered by the Bolshevists in the trenches for trying to urge their men to fight the Germans? Do they know they killed them in cold blood because the officers insisted on continuing the war, or murdered them in barracks for doing their duty? Do they know that others have been murdered in their homes for trying to protect their wives and families from the lust and brutality of the mob? Do they know that these Bolshevists have killed and starved the widows and orphans of officers and soldiers who have laid down their lives and sacrificed all for the Allied cause and their country? Are the Allies who are fighting for right and justice going to recognize and acknowledge a Government which condones such things? Are they going to help Russia to fight German influence and propaganda or to recognize a German-paid Bolshevist Government, which has betrayed Russia to the Germans and would betray the Allies too? I ask again, is England with the Allies going to recognize such a Government, a Government which has made peace with Germany? I cannot think so.

Perhaps I write too strongly, but I feel strongly. I cannot forget all those millions of officers and soldiers whom I saw gladly offering their lives for their country and their friends the Allies. In their name I write this. The only prayer of every living Russian officer and of thousands of Russian soldiers is that he may be given the chance to continue fighting the Germans and to free his country from German influence, which becomes more powerful every day and every hour. That is why the Allies should hurry on with intervention and, rejecting the idea of acknowledging traitors, form a new Allied Army throughout Siberia and other parts of Russia that will wreck the last German intrigue and will give a sure victory and peace to the world.

There is no doubt that such an Allied Army would be reinforced by many hundred thousands of Russians who in this moment cannot help and are trying, as I said before, to save their families and are waiting impatiently for help. The Allies should waste no time in this matter. If they wait much longer they may be too late.

(COLONEL) PAUL RODZIANKO
London.

I have also before me a sheet of yellowed newspaper, *The Times* of Wednesday, June 26, 1918, in which, surrounded by war news and lists of Killed, Wounded and Prisoners, is published one of my Mother's letters from Petrograd:

So many horrors have happened here that one really does not know where to begin. I thank God that you and your children are abroad. My heart is lighter knowing that some of my children have escaped these terrors.

The peasants with Bolshevic and German leaders have taken all from us. Our agents and servants in the country have barely escaped with their lives. We have been pillaged and robbed of everything. I tried to save some of the horses but they hamstrung and then burnt most of them, but your favourite horse Macgillycuddy is alive in their hands. I have sent my last roubles that I was keeping in case I had to escape from Petrograd to pay these people to leave your horse, knowing how hard it would be for you to lose him. We are now without a penny.

It is almost impossible to find food. We are starving. One can buy a few things at mad prices which we can't afford. In the streets they rob, undress and kill people, so it is terrifying to go out.

Your two youngest brothers (officers) came back from the front and are here with their wives. Your sister M. (Princess Chavchavadze) went through a frightening time in K. The Bolshevics came into her house, tied her to her bed and robbed her of everything. They would have killed her but her little daughter ran and brought help in time. Your brother Alex was commanding a brigade near Y. He tried till the last moment to make his soldiers fight but could do nothing against the Bolshevic agitators and was taken prisoner by the Germans. It is two months since I heard any news of him. Your brother Vladimir was at S. during the ghastly massacre of naval officers, but, thank God, I had a few lines from him the other day and he is still alive. Where your father is I don't know . . . They say at Constantinople.

We live here on the money we receive from the sale of household things. Otherwise we would long since be dead of hunger. No one can get any money from the banks, so God knows what future awaits us.

You can understand all this has a very bad effect on my old age. I go out very little, as in the trams the Bolshevics are so rough and rude and walking tires me so much. I wish, my dear boy, I could send you some money but I have none myself.

I cannot describe in these few words our difficult life. But we do not lose heart. God help us all—send us calm—and save us and our country from our internal enemies. Poor Russia!

One afternoon I was washing the barracks floor, which somehow did not seem to get clean. My work failed to satisfy the N.C.O., who ordered me to do it all over again. I started dismally mopping, when a voice called "No. 6285!" I was summoned to the Orderly Room, where General Knox wanted to speak to me on the 'phone. His call could not have come at a more opportune moment. Gleefully I left my bucket and scrubbing-brush.

"Hello!" came Knox's voice. "Look here, old boy, report at the War Office as soon as you can. The King has made you an Hon. Colonel and you are to join the Expeditionary Force to Siberia as a Staff Officer."

I dashed up to London, reported, and made arrangements. A few days later, having paid the children's school bills, I took my last few pounds out of the Bank and spent it on pipes and tobacco as a farewell present to the men who had been so kind to me at Tidworth. With the gifts in a large sack I got into the train for Tidworth and, tired by the last days, fell into a dead sleep. I woke up at the station past Tidworth. It was late at night and pouring rain. With a curse I shoved the sack of presents on my shoulder and started to walk back to the camp. Some yards from the station three drunken Canadians loomed up and demanded my name and destination.

"No, you're not going to Tidworth. Give us your money."

I answered rudely but felt none too easy, for many men had been robbed and murdered around the camp. One took out a knife and poked it in my ribs. "Let's kill him!"

I took this as a joke in poor taste and rather flatly asked for a match. I could think of nothing else to say, but the words were lucky. As I lit a cigarette they saw my cap and badge and began to be apologetic. In the end they helped carry my burden to a small hotel, where I spent the night.

There were many incidents of this kind and few men got off as easily as I did. When I reported the adventure at headquarters they said, "You are lucky to have got away with your life," Tidworth was a hotbed of crime during the later part of the war, it being impossible to trace thieves and murderers in a vast camp of men in identical clothing.

I distributed my presents to the men of the 10th and we had a grand farewell party. Four days later I sailed on the *Aquitania* from Southampton. Again I saw the hazy summer sky-line of New York, but this time I had more to worry about than horses, and as we steamed into harbour it seemed to me the dizzy vertical heights of skyscrapers were less impressive than the horizontal stretches of distance in Russia.

As a Colonel of the British Army I was given two lovely cabins to myself, with a bathroom, and thoroughly enjoyed five days' luxury. In New York I met my Commanding Officer, General Knox, and we crossed the continent to Vancouver on the Canadian Pacific, and from thence took the ship *Kashima Maru*. In blazing sunshine we sailed for Yokohama. The Alaskan coast shimmered in the distance, and when we were well out in the Pacific flying-fishes leapt in the green water. If it had not been for the desperate worry of our mission and the knowledge of the nightmare Revolution in Russia, it would have been the most fascinating journey. Approaching Japan we ran into a little fishing fleet, the fishermen all waving as we passed. When we arrived at Yokohama on August 23 a crowd of news reporters rushed on board clicking their cameras and trying to get an interview with General Knox. We stayed at the Imperial Hotel in Tokyo, which was later destroyed in the earthquake.

In spite of my disappointment at the European appearance of Tokyo itself, I found the rest of Japan, with its little paper houses, strange and delightful.

During our week there, we had little enough time for sightseeing. Orders had to be seen to, news sent back, regiments organized and every kind of plan made. At first I hated the feeling of rickshaws; being pulled about by a human being seemed all wrong, but in the end it was fun.

Before we left, the Japanese Minister for Defence gave a banquet in our honour at the Koyokan Restaurant. We sat on the floor with crossed legs and were served by charming little geishas. The Minister and his Staff were dressed in Samourai clothes, and our host greeted us in Japanese, which was translated by an officer. We drank a lot of *saké*, and, after a tiring day in almost unbearable heat, became very gay and happy. After serving us with many varieties of food, the geishas sat down and talked to us. They were cultivated and delightful companions and I thought maybe they resembled the hetaerae of ancient Greece. Two who spoke broken English devoted themselves to my entertainment and told me about their lives. All night the banquet went on. Beautiful costumes made the dancing interesting, but I am afraid the music was more than my untrained ear could comprehend and the singing of the lovely geishas sounded to me like cats yowling.

We walked home at dawn as the first pink light stole over the Land of the Rising Sun.

PART III

"And Since"

CHAPTER 19

The Siberian Expedition
& the Murder of the Imperial Family

THE IDEA OF foreign intervention in Siberia was to restore order and reconstitute the anti-German front in the Eastern Theatre in order to prevent further transfer of German units from the east to the west. Orders arrived for the British Military Mission under General Knox to proceed to Vladivostok. Cruisers of every nationality filled the harbour of that desolate but beautiful port. It was summer, but the Pacific beat wildly against the rocky coast as we steamed in. Two English regiments were already waiting, the Hampshire and the Middlesex Regiments, commanded by Colonel Ward, the Labour M.P. Other troops concentrated in Vladivostok included a division of Canadians, two divisions of Americans and perhaps 80,000 Japanese. The city was calm and gay, untouched as yet by Bolshevism. Races were being held and the shops were doing good trade, with the troops of several nations stationed there.

Rumours of all kinds poured in from the immense territories of Siberia, where the White Army and Cossacks were fighting Bolshevism. News came that the White Army had taken Ekaterinburg only to find the whole Imperial Family had been murdered. When the Reds knew they could hold out no longer they decided to shoot the Romanovs without trial. We later discovered that one party in the Ekaterinburg Soviet wanted to save the prisoners' lives, but the other party, headed by Goloshchokin, Yurovskikh, Safarov, Vainen and one other, determined they should be murdered. Safarov and Vainen had accompanied Lenin in his journey through Germany in 1917, so their weight probably prevailed.

Although a year had passed since the Tzar's abdication and one had ceased thinking about the Emperor in thinking about Russia, the news of the wholesale slaughter stunned. One had almost considered the Tzar dead, for what man could survive the shame of his country's plight? But now vile, if conflicting, reports leaked through of the murder of the four young Grand Duchesses and little Tzarevitch.

It was impossible, however, to get details or accurate information. No one seemed to know quite what had happened, except that before Ekaterinburg was taken the Imperial Family had disappeared.

The combined forces of Cossacks, Czechs, Poles and anti-Bolsheviks were sweeping over Siberia, flying the Independent flag of green and white that represented the snows and forests of that vast country. At every town they took the civil population greeted them with mad enthusiasm, throwing flowers and embracing each other in the streets. The Trans-Siberian railway was in our hands for 4000 miles, and all along that line "White" battalions were being formed and equipped from Vladivostok. At Omsk the Independent Siberian Government was formed under Admiral Kolchak.

As soon as the line was taken Knox ordered me to form a special train to Ekaterinburg. In four wagons guarded by Tommies of the Middlesex Regiment we arrived at Omsk after ten days through primitive wilderness, forests and plains. At each station a guard of honour was sent to General Knox by the commanders of military districts.

The Japanese soldiers in Manchuria were extraordinarily ignorant. In spite of Union Jacks plainly painted on our carriages, at Tsvarzihar they boarded the train and arrested us. Knox protested strongly and sent a wire to the High Commissioner at Vladivostok. We were lucky to get on without some sort of incident. For whom the Japanese could have mistaken us we never discovered.

The untold wealth of Siberia lies for future generations to discover and exploit.

I remember going for a walk with General Black when the train stopped by one of the stations. He picked up a stone at random: "Look at it . . . iron."

We crossed many huge rivers, some a mile wide, full of an abundance of fish; they wound through uninhabited country to the far North Ocean. The technical engineering of the bridges we passed over, most of which had been repaired after the Bolsheviks' retreat, was admirable. The beauty of the country never palled. Endless forests of great pine trees were interspersed with sheets of orange and gold, for the brilliant autumn colouring was in its full glory.

At Omsk, the big provincial town where the headquarters of the Russian Army were concentrated, we stayed several days and Knox had long discussions with Admiral Kolchak.

A few days later we steamed into the red-brick station at Ekaterinburg. Knox called me to his compartment and asked me to get a full report of the murder of the Imperial Family as quickly as possible as we had to return to Vladivostok in a few days.

A light snow was falling. Winter would soon begin. Several months having already passed since the murder, accounts were growing vaguer and more conflicting. Next morning I set out to find the people still in Ekaterinburg who might be able to give firsthand information. I was warned that those who did know anything would be too terrified to speak, and so it proved. I could get only evasive replies and shifting looks. Finally I went to Judge Sergeieff, who had taken part in the preliminary enquiries. He answered a few questions and accompanied me to the gloomy Ipatieff house where the murders had taken place.

Curiously enough, the first Romanov Tzar was offered the Crown at the Ipatieff Monastery near Moscow, and the last was murdered in this house owned by a Mr. Ipatieff in Siberia. Standing dull and isolated at the top of a street, the house was still surrounded by the wooden fence erected by the Bolsheviks to prevent the Royal Family escaping, and according to the townsfolk machine-guns had been placed on the roof so that no attempts at rescue were possible. A curious schoolboy who tried to climb the barricade was arrested and shot.

In the little yard where the family were allowed to exercise stood a wooden trestle on which the Tzar used to cut wood for the house. The former guardrooms on the top floor were now occupied by the Czechoslovak Army Staff under General Gaida. The three rooms which had been allotted the Imperial Family and the basement where the murders had taken place were kept locked and sealed. I went to General Gaida, got the keys and entered the deserted suite where Nicolas II had spent his last days. Passing through the living-room (where, Sergeieff told me, they were allowed prayers on Sundays), I came to the large room where the Emperor, Empress and Tzarevitch slept. Curiously the Empress had drawn a "swastika" beside the window, I suppose as a sign of hope. In this room there had been beds, but in the next room the four Grand Duchesses slept on mattresses on the floor. From thence a staircase led down to the basement, where the soldiers had passed the time in drinking and debauchery.

All furniture had been taken away and the cold, still emptiness of those three rooms struck a chill into one's heart. Alas, what had happened during those last six weeks was only too obvious. The Soviet of the Urals had placed the Imperial Family in the hands of a coarse, undisciplined, drunken guard. These rough men were free to vent their hatred as they pleased and took full advantage of the fact. The Tzar and his family were not allowed baths or any privacy whatsoever. A convenience of sorts existed, but not even the Empress or Grand Duchesses were allowed to go to it without a guard in attendance. Of course this was unnecessary and the men did it just to enjoy the ladies' embarrassment. During meals the guard came in and sat at the table, snatching bits of food off the plates of their captives and using obscene language, as they realized the distress their filthy talk caused. The

Romanovs took their torture quietly, however. Kings know how to die. But the Emperor's hair turned grey in a few months.

At night all doors had to be kept open and the drunken soldiers took the Grand Duchesses to the basement. Revolting inscriptions on the walls described what happened.

Then came the night when the Commissar Yurovsky, a local chemist, entered and told the Emperor that as the Whites were approaching they were all ordered to the cellar. The whole family dressed, took a few cushions on which to lie, and with their two little dogs went down the narrow staircase. Dr. Bodkin and Mademoiselle Schneider accompanied them. The moment they were all eight in the cellar Yurovsky told the Emperor that they were to be shot. The Tzar opened his mouth to plead for the children but as he spoke a bullet went through his throat, killing him outright. Then the guard began to shoot, somewhat wildly, as they were probably drunk. Until killed, the Tzarina stood firm, coldly gazing beyond this horror into that other kinder world where her battered heart had been for many months.

The maid dashed forward, desperately hitting aside the rifles with a cushion until she too fell in pools of blood. The Grand Duchess Anastasia recovered consciousness and began to scream; she was bayoneted to the floor by eighteen thrusts. Her pekinese was hit on the head, but Joy, the Tzarevitch's spaniel, hid under a chair, and next night, when the eight bodies were carried out to waiting lorries, he ran out into the streets and was picked up by an ex-officer of the Imperial Guards.

The cellar was washed, but when the Whites arrived they pulled up the floor and found masses of congealed blood, for the bodies had lain there twenty-four hours.

I examined the plaster walls in which the ricochet bullets had left their marks and counted myself the eighteen bayonet-holes in the wooden floor where the Grand Duchess Anastasia had lain.

Sergeieff told me the Tzar's beard had been cut off and for some unknown reason stuffed up the chimney. He had found it when the Commission searched the premises. Rumour had it the

Tzar's head was sent to Lenin in Moscow, but this was impossible to prove.

Unable to find any more traces or facts, I left the cold, depressing house and tried to find where the bodies had been taken to. This was not easy, for a pall of terrified silence lay over the small bleak town. Going to the Palace of Justice, I questioned the men who had taken part in the first search. Some of them told me the bodies had been taken into the forest and burnt; others said they had been buried by night in the town cemetery and that I would see a white wooden cross marked with pencil to show the place.

Next day I went to the head priest. He knew nothing, as he had not been in the town at the time. I asked permission to open the graves in his presence. Hiring some men, we went to the cemetery. I was struck by the thousands of fresh graves.

"What are all these?" I asked.

"Oh, just the townsfolk shot by the Communists," they answered. "But, sir, they are buried three and four on top of each other. It was impossible to get them in separately."

"What were so many civilians shot for?"

"Oh, just anyone who had a little money or objected to the Reds taking their possessions was shot. We had a pretty hard time last winter. It was as easy to lose your life as to drink a glass of water."

Eventually, stepping over hundreds of rough graves, we reached the white wood cross which had a pencil-mark. I ordered the men to dig. We got four bodies out, but they were decayed beyond recognition. I had hoped to be able to tell the faces, and one small body did seem rather like the Tzarevitch, but I could not be sure.

Then someone mentioned that Dr. Derevenko, who had attended the Emperor until a few days before his death, was working in Ekaterinburg Hospital. I had known him before when he was with the Tzar at headquarters at Mogilev, and sent for him immediately.

When he arrived he could only say it was impossible to identify the bodies. Suddenly an idea came to me: "Do you remember the fillings in the Tzarevitch's teeth?"

"Yes," he said, and after examining the poor little skull, proclaimed it was definitely not Alexis.

Someone suggested to try the next grave, so we dug up that one, but the result proved unsatisfactory. By now I had an idea I had been led astray and determined to cease this disgusting work. We could not examine the teeth of the thousands of corpses in the graveyard. The priest said some prayers over the bodies and we reburied them.

Apologizing for the disturbance, I left the cemetery to try a new search.

Next day I went to see General Dietrichs, Commander-in-Chief of Kolchak's army, who had just arrived. He had discovered the names of the Jews in the local Soviet who had determined that the Royal Family should be murdered, and also the names of the three who headed the shooting. He advised me to go to the village of Kopchiki, saying he had proofs that the bodies had been destroyed there.

"Do not search any more, as you won't find anything. I have special men on the job under Sokoloff. They are starting work immediately, but it will probably take months to clear the matter up."

He told me where I would find traces of the burning, and next morning, with a Russian officer as guide, I rode out to the village of Kopchiki.

For fourteen miles the sandy road led through beautiful pine trees. Five miles from the village we came to a clearing in the forest where there were some old derelict mines. Near one of them, on an open spot, was the remains of a big fire. My guide, who had been one of the first to discover the ashes, told me that according to several Bolshevik witnesses who were caught, the bodies had been carried here by lorries and the roads guarded so that no one could approach the place for several days.

By chance a little boy from the village, curious to find out what was happening in the forest, crawled through the bushes and saw a group of men working over something in this clearing. Creeping back, he told his family, and when the Whites arrived and started investigations this story reached them. Dietrichs' men had gone to the place and, raking through these ashes, they found brooches, regimental badges, pieces of corset-bone and jewels which the Empress and Grand Duchesses had sewn into the pleats of their dresses. The diamonds and emeralds were easy to identify. It was said that what fire and acid could not destroy the Reds chopped up and threw in a near-by bog. Anyway it was impossible to get further proofs.

The marks of the lorry tyres were still plainly visible but I had not time to rake through the ashes. Later on Sokoloff discovered many objects, and draining the water from the old mine they found the body of the Grand Duchess's pekinese with its skull cracked.

Dusk fell as we rode back through the lonely pine woods and I wondered much about Russia's fate. It seemed the Bolsheviks were pretty thorough in the way they did things.

Back in Ekaterinburg I went to see Sister Abaza, a nurse who had secretly tried to help the Imperial Family in every way possible. She had very nearly organized an escape, but the plans were discovered and the officers who had come to Ekaterinburg in disguise were shot. Having worked as a nurse throughout the war, Sister Abaza had followed the Tzar to Siberia, and was now working in the hospital tending wounded and sick. She met me with joy. "How good to see an old friend in these awful days!" she said, leading me into a small room where we talked. She had been a great friend of the Grand Duchess Elizabeth (sister of the Empress), and a few days previously she had discovered what had happened to the Grand Duchess, who, with the Grand Dukes Igor, Constantine, John and Serge (Inspector of Artillery) and Prince Paley, had been in captivity in the village of Alapaevsk. They were all kept in a small house with one manservant and a nun in attendance on the Grand Duchess (who since the assassination of her husband had devoted her life to religion and the poor). One evening a Commissar ordered them all to follow him out of the house. According to witnesses they asked, "Do we need to take our luggage?" The answer was "No."

Outside the village they were piled into carts and taken away into the woods. During the journey they realized they were going to their deaths. The carts stopped and they were ordered to walk a few hundred yards to some deserted mine-shafts. The Grand Duchess Elizabeth encouraged the others to sing hymns and the strange little procession advanced, their voices and the cracking of twigs the only sounds in the forest. The men walked proudly upright, the two women faltering a little in their long nun's-clothing. No wonder the mysticism of this moment, amidst dark, shivering trees, began to affect the nerves of their escort.

The Commissar ordered them to halt and announced that they were condemned to death and were to be thrown down the shaft. His voice sounded hollow and unreal. Uncomfortably his men stood by while the Grand Duchess prayed forgiveness for her murderers, then bandaging her eyes they flung her down the pit. One after another the Grand Dukes, the nun and man-servant followed.

"How did you discover all this?" I interrupted.

"Well, then a curious thing happened. The nervous strain was too much for one of the men standing by. Unable to bear the scene, he ran off into the woods and arrived home at his cottage half demented. For weeks his wife could not get a word out of him, till at last he broke down completely and confessed the story. She went to the White authorities who were searching for the Grand Duchess and told them. Soldiers went to the old mines and found the bodies at the bottom of the shaft. The Grand Duchess had been killed outright. Serge had resisted and been shot through the head. The man-servant must have lived, because he had crawled along a passage for help, and the Grand Duke John had died with his hand in the air making the sign of the cross."

Later General Dietrichs showed me the clothes; no papers had even been taken from the pockets. I also obtained photographs for the British Government. The bodies were taken to Harbin and buried, except that of the Grand Duchess Elizabeth, who had asked in her will to be buried at Jerusalem.

Sister Abaza also told me of the numerous plans for escape offered to the Emperor. The nuns in Ekaterinburg Convent supplied the Ipatieff house with milk and established a communication with the outside world by placing letters in the bottles. The Commissars never discovered these letters, but getting suddenly suspicious, stopped the milk supply.

I discovered a great deal of the Emperor's clothes and linen in the hands of private individuals all over the town. Then came news from Sergeieff that the Grand Duke Michael might be concealed in a monastery 15 miles from Ekaterinburg. I ordered some horses, jumped in a sledge and drove off. The Abbot was very suspicious of my British uniform and swore that no Grand Dukes were there. Later I discovered that Michael had been drowned in a river near Perm. The Grand Dukes Nicolas Nicolaivitch and George Constantinovitch were shot in the Petropavlovsk Fortress in Petrograd.

My week of investigations was at an end. With low spirits I returned to General Knox, gave him a report on all I had found out and what photographs I had been able to get.

Knox told me he had arranged to visit the front line 50 miles away. Next morning we arrived by train, were met by the local authorities and went to inspect the trenches. During lunch in the officers' mess I met the priest who had been allowed to say Mass in the Emperor's living-room till two days before his death. Father N—— came to my compartment in the train and we had a long talk. It was a tragic but most interesting conversation. He described the table which the Empress turned into a little altar with all her ikons, and the anguish of those services before the pale, wan faces of the family. The Commissar was always present and although he longed to give a word of comfort, the penalty was death. The Empress used to sit in a chair with the Tzarevitch on her knee. The others stood. Prayers had to be short, and when they came to kiss the cross the Emperor and Empress would softly whisper, "Thank you. Thank you."

The Empress kept her dignity to the end, growing stiffer and prouder even than she had been. The Tzar had grown a long beard and his hair had turned quite grey. "You have no idea how difficult it was to pray," the priest told me. "I had to close my eyes to keep from breaking down at the sight of that pathetic family group. I could not look at the Emperor's face; his eyes were haunted. He knew the hopelessness of their position. When the service was over, guards accompanied me out of the house, but at night I used to see their faces . . ."

The priest broke down and wept, so I could not press him further. He went back to the trenches and I never met him again.

Next day the British military train left Ekaterinburg. Staring out at the white silence of Siberian winter I saw the Tzar's kind, sad eyes and heard his voice again: "Look out for submarines . . . When you come back I will give you a Cavalry regiment to command."

CHAPTER 20

Kolchak & the End of
Allied Intervention

THE ARMISTICE WAS SIGNED. This meant the main reason for Allied Intervention, the prevention of the transfer of further German troops from the East to the West no longer held. Having encouraged the Whites, however, England realized she could not decently let them down at once. After all, the valiancy of Russia's military advance had saved Paris, marked the turning-point of the Battle of the Marne and for years prevented a German victory. The Reds had merely disorganized the Army and signed the Treaty of Brest-Litovsk. The Allies had reason to be grateful to the Russian Military Command and so in spite of general outcry in Left circles a certain measure of lukewarm intervention continued. While Kolchak's Army held the Ural front the Allied forces under General Janin (French) and General Knox were supposed to keep order without taking part in active warfare. These forces consisted of about 15,000 British soldiers, some French and Canadians, and a few Italians and Serbs. Kolchak had men but lacked statesmen and experts.

The Czech legions, anxious to return to their new country, did not fight much against Bolshevism but, well armed and well fed, they passed through Siberia, irritating the population and lording it over all who crossed their path.

For two hectic years I travelled back and forth across Siberia in the British military train with General Knox. As head of the British Mission Knox worked in collaboration with Admiral Kolchak, supervising the line of supplies. I suppose we did the 4000 miles between Vladivostok and Omsk about thirty times.

Naturally we spent a lot of time in Omsk, where the French and British Missions had headquarters, and there I met Baroness Sophie Buxhoeveden, the Empress's lady-in-waiting, who had been sent from Ekaterinburg to Perm several weeks before the White forces advanced. She was now in Omsk, which was overflowing with refugees, the population having gone up from 60,000 to 200,000. She had found lodging in the office of a man who had a room elsewhere at night. Almost every office in the town was lent at night to people who could find no other lodging. With Captain Victor Cazelet, then a member of Knox's Staff, I often visited her in her "office" after six. Sitting in our great fur coats we had long talks. When at the end of January General Knox decided to go on a journey of inspection up the line, he invited Baroness Buxhoeveden to join the military train back to Vladivostok. The journey took fourteen days, as General Knox had to stop and make many inspections. The line was constantly being attacked by bands of stray Bolsheviks, and on this trip we heard that a band of 5000 or 6000 was hiding a few miles from the line. Machineguns were prepared and our train crept in darkness through the primeval forests. Sometimes we passed for days through uninhabited country, and when we did stop, even at big places like Tomsk, the town was usually situated several miles from the railway station, as the line was built to link Vladivostok to Western Russia and not merely for the convenience of towns *en route*.

The British Tommies caused as much interest among Siberians with games of football as the Canadians did with their figure skating.

We arrived at Harbin at the time of the Chinese New Year. Tomtoms were beating and Chinese of all kinds were celebrating. From Vladivostok Baroness Buxhoeveden went back to England, and after a few weeks we started back across Siberia.

The White Army, aided by the Allies, occupied land from Vladivostok to Ekaterinburg, but the fighting went on, hard and bitter. The Reds had at their disposal all the munitions factories built up and organized during the war. As they retired they were able to use their own supplies, whereas we had but one perilous railway line across Siberia and often ran out of munitions. The White advance was successful but too hurried, for Kolchak was always over-anxious to attack the Red front line. Although a whole-hearted patriot, he gave too much time to strategy at the front, of which he knew little, and had never time for civil government in the rear, which was equally important. We also had to deal with the chaos of German prisoners pouring eastwards.

The White forces, in the vastness of Siberia, were comparatively small, and Admiral Kolchak was greatly handicapped by the shortage of good officers. His new units were trained by British officers, and in spite of the difficulties of language they did it extremely well. In fact everyone was amazed at the successful result. These 200,000 men were all equipped with British uniforms and rifles, and after three months they showed a fine performance.

"How do you like your British officers?" I asked.

"We love them, sir. We would do anything for them. They are fine fellows," the men always told me.

Meanwhile the British, American and Swedish Red Cross did invaluable work helping not only the military but the civilian population, who suffered terribly from lack of medical supplies, and from cholera and typhoid which had swept through Siberia under the Bolsheviks.

The bitter cold in winter made fighting almost impossible and we were kept huddled in Omsk during terrific snow-storms. A wedding party near Ekaterinburg got caught by wolves and was eaten, horses, bridesmaids and all.

Travelling back and forth through the winter snows and luxuriant summer green of Siberia I got a bird's-eye view of the horrors of civil war. Only the Red authorities instigated cruelties and torture, but it could not remain one-sided. Naturally the Whites retaliated on their own. The spirit of personal revenge is so deep in human nature that even military discipline cannot curb it. When our soldiers found comrades or relations mutilated they could not resist the desire to inflict suffering back. Red hate and White hate raged side by side through this beautiful wild country, so rich and so fertile, that God had given to man.

Meanwhile fronts had been formed by Generals Korniloff and Denikin in the Crimea, by Miller in the North and by Yudenitch on the West Coast. My brother Alex commanded an army with the latter forces and advanced successfully to Petrograd, but at the last moment the British refused him tanks and heavy guns.

This sort of thing caused bitter feelings among those officers who had advanced with Russia's half-ready armies in East Prussia, when England and France were shouting for an Eastern Offensive to relieve their Western front. Russia had come gallantly to the rescue, but now England was tired of fighting and decided that she did not want to "muddle herself in Russia's business."

The White Armies were short of good officers as well as of munitions. Of those who had not been killed so many could not escape from Red Russia. After two years, civil war on a vast scale still continued, although the White Armies were advancing successfully on all fronts. The outcry against intervention increased, and when Kolchak's forces were only about 300 miles from Moscow a wire came from Lloyd George in London to withdraw all British troops. This meant the British officers who had trained 200,000 Siberian soldiers so successfully were to withdraw, leaving these men with all their uniforms and failing supplies of ammunition to the mercy of the Reds.

All that two-years' effort had been wasted, 200,000 men trained and equipped at vast expense were simply stranded, because, I am wont to believe, a little Welshman and an American President did not understand the situation. The White Army that had come so far and been welcomed by the population retreated. The British officers, forced to abandon the troops who trusted them, had women in the villages shouting, "Cowards, you desert us!"

Thousands of Russian families escaped through Siberia and the British officers did their best to help them. On all the fronts I ever visited—in Russia, the Caucasus, Italy and Siberia—I had seen British officers doing their jobs, and I think I can say without prejudice that no other country has such perfect types of men in time of emergency. Whether England makes them or they have made England I do not know.

Perhaps if Kolchak had been more ruthless in putting down facetious opposition and been more of a statesman and less of an idealistic soldier he might have succeeded. He was a brave, honest, gallant gentleman.

Kolchak retired to Omsk along with many Czech forces. To the everlasting shame of his former supporters, they delivered him to the Bolsheviks in return for their own safe passage through Siberia. Kolchak was shot; this incident stands out as perhaps the greatest disgrace in modern military history.

With heavy hearts we sailed away from Vladivostok. Joy, the little ill-named spaniel who had seen his master murdered, that fateful night, travelled with me. I have never seen Russia again.

The Ipatieff House at Ekaterinburg.
The murder of the Imperial Family took place in the lower corner room
and the bodies were carried out by the doorway to left.

Bodies of the Grand Duchess Elizabeth and the Grand Dukes brought up
from the mine shaft.

Left to right: The Grand Duchess Elizabeth (as a nun) and the Grand Duchess Xenia with the Grand Duke Nicolas. Easter Celebrations, Moscow, 1913.

Training Russian Cadets for the White Army, Vladivostok, 1919. On the right in the middle distance, Rodzianko and Captain Williams.

Rodzianko with his brother Captain Serge Rodzianko.
Lucerne Horse Show, 1930.

Rodzianko as Director of the Irish Free State Cavalry School, with pupils.

CHAPTER 21

The Adventures of My Family—
I Lunch at Windsor Castle

Six months later I was in England demobilized and penniless.

During the strain of the civil war I had lost track of my family. Now in London I found my sister, who had escaped with her three children, Paul, George and Marina Chavchavadze. Arriving in England with £10 in her pocket, she immediately started painting glasses for Selfridges. Until she got a flat the Potters, grandchildren of our dear old nurse, with the greatest kindness, took them all in. Somehow she opened a dress shop and managed to educate the children well. Paul, the eldest, is now married to the daughter of the Grand Duke George Michaelovitch who was shot in Petropavlovsk Fortress, and George Chavchavadze is well known as a pianist.

Through my sister I heard that my brother Alex had finished fighting when Yudenitch's front collapsed, but Vladimir and Victor carried on under Wrangel. Serge had escaped from Petrograd on learning he was condemned to be shot, and was already playing in championship tennis tournaments in Switzerland.

My mother had happened to pass the British Embassy in Petrograd when one of the secretaries was killed by the Bolsheviks. She, an old lady, had stopped and told the crowd their behaviour was disgraceful and that one just did not treat foreign diplomats like that. Having said what she thought of them, she marched home. Soon after this, bands of rough men started coming to the house where she lived alone with a maid. They ransacked the apartments and tried to find out the whereabouts of her sons. Eventually she was arrested and put into a prison cell with many others. They had no food except what was brought from outside by friends, and no conveniences of any sort. Unable to wash she was terribly bitten by lice, especially on the hands and head.

Every day she was taken off and questioned. They tried to get information out of her by telling her we had been caught and shot, but she gave away nothing. Eventually she was condemned to death, but by great good luck Victor's Swiss tutor got his Ambassador, who was leaving Petrograd, to go to the Bolshevik authorities and insist on taking Mother with him. She often describes the curious sensation of that last night, praying and waiting to be taken out and shot. Then the key turned, she stood up prepared to die and was hurriedly told to collect her belongings as the Swiss Ambassador was waiting. Mother's charm had won the heart of her gaoler and the man tried to be kind to her. Baroness Meyendorff, imprisoned with her, describes the poor man's horror when Mother seized his hand to say good-bye and loudly exclaimed, "My dear man, whatever happens I hope you get made a General!"

During the fighting in the Crimea my brother Victor had stuck to a battery and continued firing when the other men were killed. He was wounded in the back and finally rescued by an American officer who got him onto a destroyer and brought him to Constantinople to be operated on. Nadia, his wife (the daughter of General Bezobrazov), had a terrible time getting out of Russia on her own. Eventually she met Victor by chance in the streets of Constantinople. Victor worked his way to U.S.A. as a stoker, and the same officer who had saved his life helped him to get a job in New York.

Father had left Wrangel's Army and escaped through Constantinople. Sasha Chavchavadze, my brother-in-law, was still fighting in his beloved Georgia.

This was the story of my family. Incredibly they had all managed to escape in different ways and different directions. It would take volumes to write of the extraordinary tragedies, horrors and adventures that befell my friends and other relations. Hairbreadth escapes from Russia continue until this day and the world is tired of them. It is harder to leave the country now, but in the turmoil of revolution many of my friends got out by mere fluke. One of them condemned to be shot with a line of others fell unhit and afterwards crawled away. Europe is bored with Russian bestiality and cruelty, but half the tales remain unrecorded. It will take the dazed world many years to realize the full tragedy of our Revolution. I myself cannot believe that I have lived through and witnessed such things.

Many officers, home-sick for their own country, went back and joined the Russian Army. They have almost all been shot. I was myself approached by a Bolshevik agent to return and train the Cavalry. Apparently the idea was to restore some efficiency to the Army and then bump off the experts when they had no longer any need for them. That is not, however, the way to build up confidence in a body of men. All that the Soviet achieved in the fifteen years after the Revolution they have destroyed in the last five. I am sorry for Russia's allies in the next war; they will shout for help in vain.

Sasha Chavchavadze stayed in Georgia until 1930, when the Bolsheviks shot him. He was a gallant and fearless soldier, adored by the men he led, as chivalrous as he was brave. His sons and grandson proudly carry on his name.

For the first time in my life I was out of an army and had to look around for a way of "making money." I had tried many things in my life, but never that. In fact I was as innocent about finance as a convent demoiselle should be about love.

My only talent lay in the equestrian line, so buying a charming little place at Windsor with stabling and a covered school, I started training horses and riders. It was a grand life. I had over thirty horses in the stables, and apart from the *entourage* of Windsor, pupils came to me from all over England. The Prince of Wales and the King of Greece often came to ride, and the former had a gate made straight from my place into Windsor Park. What times they were! My house was always crammed with people; every day I had ten to twenty for tea and drinks. Keeping open house and riding and training all day, I was too tired to attend to bills and that side of the question was ignored.

One day King George invited me to lunch at Windsor Castle to hear my account of the Siberian Expedition and of the murders of his cousins. I arrived at the Castle in pouring rain, clad in my old trench mackintosh and on a motor bicycle, my only means of transport. It was a quarter to one. The sentry looked me up and down and refused to let me enter.

"I am lunching with the King and will be late," I pleaded.

"Tell me another," he grinned.

Finally I left the motor bicycle at the White Hart Hotel and, looking as respectable as possible, was allowed cautiously through the gates. I lunched alone with Their Majesties and of course discussed the painful subject of the murders in Ekaterinburg. The King wanted to know details which I was loath to give him, the episode was so intimate. I described the cold, empty rooms and blood-stained cellar of the Ipatieff house, my fruitless search in the graveyard and the grim ride through the Siberian forest to find a patch of ashes. I told him frankly all I knew, but it was naturally a somewhat painful conversation.

I was in the midst of a harrowing description when the most revolting dish of what looked like rotten grey eggs in jelly was offered me: "What on earth is this?" I blurted out.

"Plovers' eggs," said the King; "a great delicacy."

After lunch His Majesty showed me the pictures, and I told them of "Joy," who ran about my garden. He seemed quite happy, but staring into those limpid brown eyes I often wondered how much he could remember.

Eight years at Sefton Lawn passed like a week. The most amusing people were entertained, but although I was successful with horses this did not increase my income.

My horse Zorab had been taken prisoner by the Germans during the war. My brother Alex, also a German prisoner, got him back after the Armistice and eventually returned him to me. After six years of adventure he was still a brilliant jumper and I won a number of competitions on him. He jumped over 7 feet in my riding school.

When the depression came I had to sell my place and move away. It was sad after eight years of happy English life, among the kindest and most charming people. I had been so busy that I had hardly noticed that my children had suddenly and disconcertingly grown up. From being imps that one spanked and put to bed they turned into two definite personalities with wills and ideas of their own.

In 1928 I found myself without home or money in London, the city where I had once enjoyed such glory (or so it seemed). The famous Rosa Lewis, always kind to the down-and-out, came to my rescue; a sort of Robin Hood of Mayfair, she invited me to her hotel, where I stayed six months until I managed to make enough to pay her. She was actually surprised at getting the money.

I went off to Leicestershire to train horses at East Langton, and for six months I enjoyed the world's most wonderful hunting. I am afraid I got laughed at sometimes because I had to train horses, not just ride, and even when hounds were running I sometimes popped back over a jump to take it better. Hunting in the Midlands is one of the most exciting things in the world. The Compagna Romana is bigger but different; it has not the same thrill as a good day's hunting in England.

My brother Serge, as well as playing in international lawn-tennis tournaments, had been riding in Continental Horse Shows and now he appeared in Leicestershire to ride horses for various people. Although a beautiful rider he was rather cowed by the English huntin' women, who cursed him at gates and told him to "Shut up, we're hunting," if he spoke when hounds ran. Serge had a horse, Rosalynd, that he trained to jump without reins. At Vienna Horse Show he gave an exhibition but unfortunately on this occasion Rosalynd did not stop. Having jumped the course once, she went on around and around while poor Serge "whoa-ed" in vain and his friends roared with laughter.

CHAPTER 22

Conclusions

I WAS BACK AT the Cavendish Hotel training Major Dudgeon of the Scots Greys for the King's Cup (which he won), when a letter arrived from Colonel Hogan of the Irish Free State Army asking me to come over to Dublin.

I had not been in Ireland since going there to buy horses with the Italian Commission. I had bought fifty for my regiment at the same time, and the memory of our tour through the flat big-banked fields of Meath and Waterford and Clare was still with me.

Colonel Hogan met me at Kingstown in the grey light of dawn. I spent several days in Dublin with him discussing propositions and finally the Minister for Defence nominated me Director of the Cavalry School.

The Irish Show Jumping Team had splendid horses, great courage and a certain amount of experience but no technical knowledge. I met the officers and started training them right away. After two weeks they won the Aga Khan's Cup at Dublin International Show. It was a good start.

For four years I lived in Dublin what must be the most delightful and care-free military life in the world. We did not start work at 6 A.M. as in Italy, but I usually got my "boys" to the riding school at 10 A.M., and what grand material they were! With Irish horses and Irish hearts I knew I ought to win all round the world, and sure enough my pupils soon became one of the leading teams of Europe.

As a Russian I found a great similarity between the Irish peasants and those of my own country, the same touch of poetry, philosophy and cruelty; the same charming way of discarding logic and getting straight to the point. What I could not quite understand was the bitter difference between Protestant and Catholic. Soon after I arrived, in Dublin a friend asked if I could get his horse trained in a certain place. I asked and was amazed at the refusal on the grounds it was a Protestant horse!

And then the hunting! I had seen fine cross-country riding in Italy and Leicestershire but never will I forget the amazing performances, in Meath, of untrained young horses, ridden by some farmer's lout with string for reins. They would vanish over banks that made me stop and think! In Italy no one ever thought of going out hunting on a horse that was not perfectly trained. In England I had been surprised by the, to me, unnecessary foolhardiness of riders risking their necks on horses who did not know how to jump. But I had seen nothing like the performances of young horses in the really big country of Meath and the Ward Union, nor the amount of falls that riders seemed prepared to take. It seemed to me a pity to take such risks.

Occasionally I was rather puzzled at getting orders written in Gaelic which even my Adjutant, who had studied, was hard put to it to translate. During one of my leaves in England I was training Lord Gough, Commander of the Irish Guards, when he fell at a jump and broke his knee. Back in Dublin a few weeks later I got a pompous letter from the War Office asking me to describe the accident, as Lord Gough would be in hospital several months. As Director of the Irish Cavalry School I decided to send the answer in Gaelic and got a Professor to write out a fine report to which I signed my name. I believe the War Office sent the document to the British Museum to be deciphered!

After four grand years I returned to England and trained officers at Aldershot. One day I could not get the Scots Greys to push their horses fast enough. Tired of shouting, I had a new idea and yelled, "Charge as you did at Waterloo!" It was incredible a body of men could change so quickly. They went like smoke.

Apart from my Irish Team I now had several very good English pupils, Major Joe Dudgeon and Captain Mike Ansell being among the best. During the Show season a pupil, Captain Fanshaw of the 16th Lancers, asked me to help him win the Duke of Connaught's Cup at Olympia. He was engaged to a very pretty girl, so I told him I would do my best, and that would be my wedding present to him. He won it.

A pretty bad moment came once when I was training young officers. While I was working an officer from another regiment came to jump, fell and was rolled on. The ambulance took an hour to arrive and he died before the doctors even saw him. Military hospitals are sometimes rather strange. A friend of mine who shall be nameless went to have his appendix out. The stretcher broke on the way to the operating room but they got him there somehow and then took his tonsils out by mistake! In the summer of 1935 I fell while training regimental officers. On being assured nothing was broken, I went on riding and training for two weeks, feeling queer and faint. At last I was X-rayed in London and it was found that my collar-bone was broken and was pressing on an artery.

It is amusing to look back on my varied career. I remember the old, unbelievable court life in Petrograd; the grand men of my regiment and the evenings when the singers came in walking on their hands. I also remember with bitterness the way those men fought and died—for what?

Then I think of Paris in 1904 with the world's prize cocottes strolling the boulevards and the Moulin Rouge crowded with silk hats and long gowns pinned with dazzling jewels (no courtesan would have shamed herself by wearing false ones). The other day I visited the city again, a gloomy, frightened Paris, obsessed by strikes, hysterically discussing the next war. Painted but depressed women sat at the cafés, grim reality in their eyes. To them life was no longer a mad dream. I strolled into an unrecognizable Moulin Rouge where little shop-girls danced drearily with shabby young men. A fifth-rate, pathetically cheap cabaret appeared. There was no wine, no laughter, glamour or wit to relieve the sordid atmosphere.

And so much is like that. Something wild and care-free and joyous has gone out of human life. I am sorry for young people, for a gay youth is something that all the bitterness of later life can never take away.

Yet working hard with horses, riding and training all day, I have little enough time to look backwards and the speed of modern events forces one to look forward. Europe again stumbles towards the melting-pot and this green, unhurried life in England may not last for ever. Every time I pass my garden at Windsor I think of the small dog's tomb in the bushes with the ironical inscription "Here lies Joy." To me that little stone marks the end of an empire and a way of life.

Yet Russia remains. My children still dream and talk of Russia. Their blood remains Russian blood; they are but exiles, foreigners in a kindly country. A young man comes to see me. Brought up under the Soviet, he has no remembrance or knowledge of what life there was before. He is the new generation. He has toiled as a peasant, slaved in Leningrad, been cold and hungry, lost a leg in a concentration camp and somehow escaped.

"I never knew what luxury was," he says, "until by mistake I was put in a Commissars' Nursing Home in Moscow. Then I saw a new class of people of whose existence I had not dreamed. They ate grapes and their children visited them in limousines and how fat those children were!"

"Never mind," I comfort him, "batches of Commissars have been shot off lately."

And we talk of Russia's soul. After two years in the "paradise of London" he still yearns for that country to which we belong. "Until I went into the hospital," he tells me, "I had never had quite enough to eat, and when they let me out and I walked down the streets for the first time I wondered how the people could stand it, and then, I remembered, I too had been like them, dull, listless, too tired to revolt. For twenty years the masses have had their noses to the grind-stone, obsessed by the struggle not to be shot, to get just enough to eat and a place to sleep. Too little food and too much work have worn the spirit out of them."

And then he says a curious thing, contradicting what many visitors and foreigners say of Russia: "Too exhausted to rebel, the people remain hungry for spiritual relief. Turning away from the terrible materialism of everyday life, they pave the way for a great religious revival. The only places in Russia where words of philosophy and love are spoken are the churches. Therefore in spite of persecution they are crowded, for even the young turn desperately in search of beauty and only there can they find it. Cant and slogans do not really satisfy. Stronger even than the desire for food and clothing is the desire for belief and peace."

I meet many older Russians of every class and profession who have got out in the last few years and they speak of other things, of growing Anti-Semitism, of peasant revolts and villages wiped out with poison gas. Things which no newspaper ever records; but this youth, moulded by the Soviet machine, interests me more for he is the new generation, crept out into a different world.

I cannot believe that Russia's spirit is broken and that she will remain grim and dull, for the people are born of her black soil and sweet-smelling forests and sweeping plains, not of political systems. Beyond the towns and factories and communal institutions, Russia must remain the same.

Perhaps Revolution teaches and the thousands of men who died fighting like tigers will leave a rich heritage to their sons, for what is in the hearts of brave men does not die but lives on in the hearts of others, white and eternal as Russia's snows.

CPSIA information can be obtained
at www.ICGtesting.com
Printed in the USA
LVHW02s0546170518
577472LV00003B/3/P